FORTY YEARS

AT

EL PASO

1858—1898

RECOLLECTIONS OF WAR, POLITICS, ADVENTURE, EVENTS, NARRATIVES, SKETCHES, ETC.

BY

W. W. MILLS

"Around my fire a friendly group to draw
And tell of all I felt and all I saw."

...TO...

MARY HAMILTON MILLS

Marula
An imprint of Arcadia Publishing

Forty Years at El Paso: 1858–1898
by Walker C. Smith

A Marula Historical Reprint
Originally published in 1901

Published by Arcadia Publishing
Charleston SC

ISBN 978-0-7385-9459-0

Printed in the United States of America

For all general information contact Arcadia Publishing at:
Telephone 843-853-2070
Fax 843-853-0044
E-mail sales@arcadiapublishing.com
For customer service and orders:
Toll-Free 1-888-313-2665

Visit us on the Internet at www.arcadiapublishing.com

A WARNING.

These writings are meant to be truthful, but they are too rambling and egotistical to possess much historical value. Few subjects are treated of except such as the writer was personally connected with or in which he felt a special interest. Much that he was tempted to write has been omitted out of consideration for the living and the dead and their relations.

The book will have little interest except for those who know something of El Paso or of the men and events treated of, or of the writer himself.

For such only is it written.

W. W. MILLS.

El Paso,
November, 1901.

CONTENTS.

Forty Years at El Paso.

I was born on a farm near Thorntown, Indiana, in 1836, and labored alongside of my father and brothers and the hired men during the crop season, attending the village school during the winter months, till I was seventeen years old, when my father sent me for two years to an academy in New York State. While there he secured for me an appointment as a cadet at the Military Academy at West Point, but I gave way to my brother, Anson Mills, who is now a Brigadier General in the United States army. After returning home for a year, I came to Texas with my brother Anson. We came down the Mississippi at the time of the great flood in 1857, to New Orleans, and thence up the Red River to Jefferson, Texas. From Jefferson we walked to McKinney, in Collin County, where my brother had previously resided, and I secured a school at Pilot Grove, in Grayson County, and spent a year there happily, and, I trust, usefully. During that year my brother was appointed surveyor on the part of Texas to the joint commission which located the boundary line between Texas and the United States, Col. William R. Scurry being the commissioner on the part of Texas.

At the suggestion of my brother, I joined this expedition at Horsehead Crossing on the Pecos River, and accompanied it to El Paso. When we arrived at Waco Tanks, twenty-six miles east of El Paso, we failed to find water, and were somewhat distressed in consequence.

Colonel Scurry said that young men on foot could make the trip to El Paso for relief better than any of our worn-out animals, and my brother and I volunteered for the tramp. We left the tank, thirsty, at sunset and reached the river below El Paso before daybreak, and after slaking our thirst, slept on the ground till morning, when we sent out a relief party, with water. Soon thereafter I went to Fort Fillmore, in New Mexico, forty-five miles above El Paso, where I clerked in the sutler's store of Hayward & McGrosty, for nearly a year, when I returned to El Paso, and was employed in the same capacity by St. Vrain & Co., merchants. This firm had a branch store at the Santa Rita copper mines near where Silver City now stands, and I made two journeys to and from that place, the first time on horseback and alone. There was no habitation between La Messilla and Santa Rita, and the country was full of hostile Indians; but of them later on. I remember camping alone over night at the place now known as Hudsons Hot Springs. The second journey I made as wagonmaster of our train laden with merchandise for the Santa Rita store, and brought back a load of copper, which we sent by wagons to Port La Vaca, eight hundred miles, and thence to New York by Gulf and Sea.

While at the copper mines, three prospectors—Tayor, Snively and another—came to my camp and reported that they had discovered placer gold at Pinos Altos, near there, and, as they were out of provisions and money, I gave them what was called a "grub stake"—that is, provisions to continue their explorations. That was in 1859, and I am told that gold is still being washed out at Pinos Altos, in 1900.

EL PASO IN 1858.

El Paso is situated on the Rio Grande River, in the extreme west corner of Texas, within a mile of that river, which forms the boundary line between Texas and Mexico, and very near to New Mexico on the north and on the west.

The altitude is 3,700 feet and the climate is mild, pleasant and healthful. El Paso was then a small adobe hamlet of about three hundred inhabitants, more than three-fourths of whom were Mexicans. Nearly all that portion of the village or "ranch" south of San Antonio and San Francisco streets was then cultivated in vineyards, fruit trees, fields of wheat and corn and gardens, for at that time and for years later there was an abundance of water in the Rio Grande all the year round, and El Paso was checkered with acequis (irrigation ditches).

At the head of El Paso street, near the little plaza, where the main acequia ran, there were several large ash and cottonwood trees, in the shade of which was a little market where fruit, and vegetables, and fowls, and mutton, and venison, and other articles were sold. We had no regular meat market.

To one of these trees some enterprising citizen had nailed a plank, which for years served as a bulletin board where people were wont to tack signed manuscripts giving their opinions of each other. Here Mrs. Gillock, who kept the hotel where the Mills building now stands, notified the "Publick" when her boarders refused to pay their bills, and here, in 1859, I saw my brother

Anson nail the information that three certain citizens were liars, etc., and here, just ten years later, I gave the same information regarding B. F. Williams. Foolish? Perhaps.

The flouring mill of Simeon Hart, about a mile above the village, was the chief individual industrial enterprise in the valley, and ground the entire wheat crop from both sides of the river, and supplied flour to all the people and the military posts.

The proprietor, a man of wealth and influence, staked all and lost all in the Confederate cause.

The dam which supplied water to this mill had been constructed two hundred years ago by the people of the Mexican side of the river, who kept it in repair for all these years without asking any assistance from the people of the Texas side, although they generously divided the water with us.

The patience and industry displayed by this people in repairing and rebuilding this dam, when washed away by annual floods, can only be compared to that of beavers.

The Texas bank of the Rio Grande was then (1858) only a short distance south of where the Santa Fe depot now stands, but just how far south it is impossible for me or any one else, I believe, to tell, though I have been often asked to testify as to where the river bed was then, and in later years. It found its present bed more or less gradually by erosion and revulsion during these years, and left very few landmarks.

The bed of the river was narrower then than now, and many cottonwood trees grew upon each bank.

At the end of El Paso street was the ferry, where pedestrians crossed in small canoes, and vehicles and wagon trains in larger boats.

Sometimes, when the spring floods came, it was impossible for any one to cross for several days.

Be it remembered there was not a railroad or telegraph station within a thousand miles of us. The business houses, with one exception, were on El Paso street, and around the little plaza. My brother Anson and I each built homes at El Paso before the war, he on San Francisco and I on San Antonio street. The postoffice was on the west side of El Paso street, facing the head of San Antonio street, and in this same large room there was also a whiskey saloon, a billiard table, and several gambling tables. "Uncle Ben" Dowell was postmaster. This room and the street in front of it were the favorite shooting grounds of the sporting men, and others, and here took place many bloody encounters, some of which may be treated of in these idle writings. The graveyard was convenient, being on one of the hills on what is now known as "Sunset Heights." At one time there were more people buried there who had died by violence than from all other causes. When I state that the writer of these pages sometimes read the burial service there over the remains of our departed countrymen, it may be imagined how sadly we were in need of spiritual guidance. Every citizen, whatever his age or calling, habitually carried a six-shooter at his belt, and slept with it under his pillow. I remember a friend, Johnnie Evans, saying to me once, when I was so thoughtless as to start down street without one: "Buckle it on, Mills; we don't often need 'em, but when we do need 'em, we need 'em—Oh, God!" Every man's horse, or team, and arms were the best his purse could buy, and my white saddle horse, that carried me for ten years, was surely a dandy. Sometimes, when I have journeyed to Las Cruces or Mesilla, fifty miles, in my buggy, I have turned this animal loose, saddled and bridled, and he has followed me the whole distance, as a dog follows his master. I have sometimes been vexed with the best of my human friends, but "Blanco" never disappointed me in anything.

The Mexican population, now nearly all passed away by death or removal, were of a much better class than those who came in later with the advent of the railroads, to sell their labor—and their votes. It is but just to say, however, that votes cannot be sold unless there be purchasers, and that the purchasers have ever been of my own race.

The villages below El Paso were more prosperous then than now, because their population is agricultural and the lack of water in the river in recent times has caused great discouragement and even distress. The same was true of Juarez Mexico, just opposite El Paso, then called Paso del Norte.

The county seat was first at San Elezario, twenty-two miles below El Paso, with fifteen hundred population, and later at Ysleta, with twelve hundred population (nearly all Mexicans), and still later at El Paso. Court proceedings and arguments to juries and political speeches were then made in the Spanish language.

Fort Bliss, garrisoned by regular United States troops, situated at the place now called East El Paso, was considered by army officers and their families as one of the most desirable posts in the whole country, and several officers who subsequently held very high rank during the Civil War had been stationed there. There was another fort, called Quitman, seventy miles below El Paso, on the river, and a chain of military posts from there to San Antonio. The nearest posts in New Mexico were Fort Fillmore, forty miles to the north, near Las Cruces, and

Fort Craig, one hundred miles still further north toward Santa Fe.

As to hunting, there were at that time comparatively plenty of wild deer, turkeys, wild geese, ducks and mountain quail on the mountains and in the valley, and I got my share of them.

ROSTER OF ANTE-BELLUM RESIDENTS OF EL PASO.

J. F. Crosby, then district judge, Confederate; is well known in El Paso.

Simeon Hart, mill owner and contractor, Confederate. Died at El Paso.

Henry J. Cuniffe, merchant, Union man. Was United States Consul at Juarez. Died at Las Cruces.

H. S. Gillett, merchant and Confederate, lives in New Mexico.

J. S. Gillett, merchant, Confederate; lives in New Mexico.

Col. Phil Herbert, lawyer, Confederate; killed in the war.

Col. James W. Magoffin, contractor, Confederate; sutler at Fort Bliss. Died at San Antonio.

Joseph Magoffin, Confederate; served in the war; now lives in El Paso.

Sam Magoffin, Confederate; killed in the war.

Anson Mills, engineer, Union; now brigadier general, U. S. A. Lives in Washington, D. C.

W. W. Mills, clerk, Union; served in the war; now United States Consul at Chihuahua, Mexico.

Emmett Mills, Union; killed in Indian fight in Arizona in 1861.

Samuel Schutz, merchant and Union man; now in El Paso.

Joseph Schutz, merchant, Union; died in 1895.

Col. George H. Giddings, manager San Antonio Mail Co.

H. C. Hall, agent San Antonio Mail Co.

Capt. Henry Skillman, frontiersman, Confederate; killed in the war.

Brad Daily, Union scout and spy; died at Las Cruces, N. M.

Col. Hugh Stephenson, mine owner and merchant; lived and died at Concordia, near El Paso.

Uncle Billy Smith, patriarch of the valley; thrown from stage coach at El Paso in 1860 and killed.

Vicente St. Vrain, merchant, Union; died in New Mexico.

A. B. O'Bannon, deputy collector customs, Confederate; dead.

William Morton, district attorney, Confederate; dead.

Charles Merritt, manager Hart's mill; dead.

Henry C. Cook, lawyer, Confederate; dead.

B. S. Dowell, postmaster, Confederate; died at El Paso.

Nim Dowell, Union; killed by Confederates in Texas.

Fred Percy, English gentleman, Confederate; dead.

Rufus Doane, county surveyor; dead.

Billy Watts, sheriff; dead.

Emilio Deuchesne, merchant, Union; died in 1895, in Juarez.

Russ Howard, lawyer, Confederate; now in San Antonio.

A. B. Rohman, merchant; dead.

R. L. Robertson, agent Overland Mail Company, Union; dead.

Dr. Nangle, agent San Antonio Mail Company, Union; dead.

James Buchanan, merchant in Juarez; dead.

Charles Richardson, Confederate; lives in Juarez.

D. R. Diffendorffer, merchant in Juarez.

F. R. Diffendorffer, merchant in Juarez.

G. W. Gillock, justice of the peace and hotel-keeper; dead.

J. E. Terry, with the stage company; lives in El Paso.

Charles Music, merchant; lives in Mexico; and

Andrew Hornick, H. McWard, George Lyles, —— Tibbits, —— Milby, David Knox, Bill Conklin and Tom Miller.

There were usually about a dozen United States army officers at old Fort Bliss, now East El Paso.

The most prominent Mexican citizens in Paso del Norte (now Juarez) were:

Dr. Mariano Samaniego, Inocente Ochoa, José M. Flores, all still residing in Juarez; José M. Uranga, Jefe Politico, dead; Juan N. Zubiran, collector of customs, my partner and friend; and the venerable Ramon Ortiz, who ministered there as curate for fifty years, and died a few years since, beloved of the two races.

The Americans living at Ysleta and San Elizario before the war were: Price Cooper, Henry Corlow, Tom Collins, Henry Dexter, James McCarty, A. C. Hyde, William Claude Jones; and Fred Pierpoint, who died of hydrophobia at El Paso in 1869.

Of those named above as residing at El Paso in 1860, the following left with the retreating Texans in 1862: Crosby, Hart, the Gilletts, the Magoffins, Herbert, Merritt, O'Bannon, Morton, Cook, Skillman, Dowell, Richardson and Russ Howard. Some of the last named remained away for years and others never returned.

In their places there came soon (mostly discharged Union officers and soldiers): A. H. French, J. A. Zabriskie, G. J. Clarke, E. A. Mills, Nathan Webb, A. J. Fountain, William P. Bacon, Edmond Stein, S. C. Slade, John

Evans, George Rand, Joe Shacker, Solomon Schutz, Louis Cardis, and Charles H. Howard.

Except those last named, there was but little increase in the American population of El Paso for about fifteen years.

INCIDENTS BEFORE THE WAR AND EARLY IMPRESSIONS.

On the second night after my arrival in El Paso I had my first experience of the manner of settling difficulties there. Samuel Schutz, still of El Paso, and one Tom Massie had had a misunderstanding about the rent of a house. My brother and I went across the river that afternoon, and on the way we met one Garver, a half-witted fellow, called "Clown," who said he had been "fixing a canoe" at the river, and in a friendly way he advised us to return early because there would be some fun that night. We asked him what fun, and he replied: *"Oh, killin' a Dutchman!"* That night, in front of the postoffice, I heard Massie say to a friend: "I have taken half a dozen drinks of straight brandy, but d—n me if I can get drunk." I went into the postoffice and found an unusual crowd of men talking in low tones, and Mr. Schutz, in his shirt sleeves, was playing billiards with a friend. Presently Massie entered, and saying, "Mr. Schutz, you told a d—d lie," presented a cocked pistol at that gentleman. There was no mistaking his intention. Murder was in his voice and in his face. Then there came from Mr. Schutz such a sound as I never heard before or since. It was not a shriek, or an outcry, for he did not distinctly articulate a single word. It was not exactly an expression of fear, but was more like a prolonged wail over some tragedy which had already occurred. But Schutz did the right thing, and quickly. He seized the barrel of Massie's pistol and held it upward. Then commenced a struggle for life. Both were powerful men, and in their prime, one moved by hatred and revenge, and the other by the instinct of self-preservation. It was some seconds after they grappled before that strange sound ceased. Massie strove to bring his cocked pistol to bear on Schutz, and Schutz to move it in any other direction. Shocked and alarmed, and remembering my teaching about law and order, I stepped forward and said, "Gentlemen, would you see the man murdered?" *Not a man moved.* Massie finally let fall his pistol, drew a knife and drove it into Schutz's shoulder. Schutz fled, but Massie recovered his pistol and fired two shots at him as he ran out through the front door. It was dark outside. Immediately after the shots Schutz stumbled over a water barrel and fell, and Massie, thinking him dead, crossed to Mexico in that canoe which Clown had "fixed." Schutz was untouched by the bullets, and the knife wound was not serious.

The next day "Uncle Ben" Dowell gave me this advice: "My young friend, when you see anything of that kind going on in El Paso, don't interfere. It is not considered good manners here." The advice was well intended and worthy of careful consideration. Tom Massie returned to El Paso, but was not prosecuted.

Not long after the above occurrence, I saw a certain gambler shooting at another member of the profession in this same postoffice. A stray bullet killed an inoffensive by-stander. The coroner's jury exonerated the killer, as they said the killing was clearly "accidental." There was, of course, some sympathy for the innocent dead man, but most of it appeared to go to the gambler who had been so "unfortunate" as to kill *the wrong man.*

Of the Americans then at El Paso, some had left wives, or debts, or crimes behind them in "the States," and had not come to the frontier to teach Sunday school. But there were good people here also, and for the few who were capable of doing business and willing to work, the opportunities were as good then and as profitable as they have ever been since that time. The products of the mines, crudely worked, in northern Mexico, were brought to El Paso and exchanged for merchandise or money. The military posts (forts) in northwest Texas and southern New Mexico were supplied with corn, flour, beef, hay, fuel, etc., by El Paso merchants and contractors.

The Overland Mail Company then operated a weekly line of mail coaches, drawn by six animals, between St. Louis and San Francisco. The time between these two cities was usually twenty-six days, the distance being 2,600 miles. These splendid Concord coaches (now almost gone out of use) carried the United States mail, for a Government subsidy, and usually four to nine through passengers, besides the driver and "conductor." Changes of animals were made at "stations" built of rock or adobe, every twenty-five to forty miles, or wherever the company could find a stream, or spring, or water-hole. These coaches traveled day and night, in all kinds of weather.

El Paso was at this time (1858) the terminus of two other important stage routes—one from Santa Fe, New Mexico, and the other from San Antonio, Texas. These were in every particular so similar to the greater "Overland" route that a description is unnecessary. There was also a stage line to Chihuahua.

These mail coaches were the forerunners of the "Limited Express" and the Pullman sleeper of the present day; and the rough, brave men who drove and managed them and protected the stations, fighting Indians the while, were the pioneers, the Daniel Boones and Simon Kentons of this frontier! They opened the way for the Southern Pacific, the Mexican Central, the "Sunset" and the Santa Fe.

Does the tenderfoot who now rides over these routes, in luxury and safety, appreciate the work of these men? I have heard more than one of them intimate that he would have done things much better than we did, if he had only arrived in time. I am very sure I have heard several of them say that they would have made and saved plenty of money, if they had only had our opportunities; and this appears to me the proper place for a few remarks on success and failure in life; if, indeed, any place is good for such a homily. By success I, of course mean what the majority of men mean by the word success—the accumulation of wealth.

Well, during the ten years following my locating at El Paso, I was well and familiarly acquainted with at least fifty active, intelligent, educated young men, of whom it might have been predicted that they would succeed in life. These, if now living, would all have more than three-score years. Several of them died by the hands of the Indians, and some of them by the hands of their own countrymen, a number went to the bad or died early. Several of them lived beyond middle age and led brave, honorable and useful lives, but I recall *only two* who could be classed as successful men, according to the above test. True, some of them gained much money and spent it liberally and often charitably, or lost it, but according to the popular idea, a man to be successful must have plenty of money *when he dies.* And though he leaves no minor children or dependents, his neighbors will whisper at his funeral, "He died poor," in much the same tone as one might say, "He was hanged."

In order that the importance of these mail routes and

other enterprises on this frontier may be appreciated, I must here state a fact which may seem strange to some of my readers. At that time this whole frontier was in the actual possession of savage Indians. The Americans and Mexicans were secure only near the military posts, or villages, or large settlements, and when they traveled from place to place, they traveled in companies strong enough for defense, or at night and by stealth, trusting to Providence, or luck, each according to his faith.

The men who, for whatever reasons, had made their way to this distant frontier, were nearly all men of character; not all of good character, certainly, but of positive, assertive individual character, with strong personality and self-reliance. (The weaklings remained at home.) Many of them were well bred and of more than ordinary intelligence, and maintaining the manners of gentlemen. Even the worst of these men are not to be classed with the professional "toughs" and "thugs" who came later with the railroads. They were neither assassins nor thieves nor robbers. Vices? Plenty; but they were not of the concealed or most degrading kinds. Violence? Yes, but such acts were usually the result of sudden anger or of a feeling that under the conditions then existing each man must right his own wrongs or they would never be righted. Their ideas of right and wrong were peculiar, but they *had* such ideas nevertheless. I knew a young man who was well liked and had good prospects, who violated confidence and attempted to betray his benefactor. The facts became known. Now, if he had shot a man because he did not like him much, anyhow, or if he had run away with his neighbor's wife, his conduct might have been overlooked. But treachery? Ingratitude? Never! He became the most despised man in the community. The merchants and business men were certainly an exceptional class. Honorable, highly intelligent, charitable and gentlemanly. I could name a dozen gentlemen who were here even as far back as the "sixties," from which list I believe any President might have selected an able cabinet. Not all of these were of my own race; and yet, even these did not hold themselves entirely aloof from the other classes. The times did not favor or permit such exclusiveness.

Common trials and dangers united the two races as one family, and the fact that one man was a Mexican and another an American was seldom mentioned, and I believe as seldom thought about. Each man was esteemed at his real worth, and I think our estimates of each other's characters were generally more correct than in more artificial societies.

Spanish was the language of the country, but many of our Mexican friends spoke English well, and often conversations, and even sentences, were amusingly and expressively made up of a blending of words or phrases of both languages.

To the traveler, who had spent weeks crossing the dry and desert plains, this valley, with the grateful humidity of the atmosphere, the refreshing verdure, the perfume of the flowering shrubs, the rustling of the leaves of the cottonwood trees, and their cool shade, and in the spring or summer, the bloom of the many fruit trees, or the waving of grain fields, were all like a sight or breath of the Promised Land!

The people, the peasantry, were content and happy. To them, with their simple wants, it was a land of plenty. The failure of water in the Rio Grande has sadly changed all this. It may be said that this valley and the things here described were not in themselves beautiful, but only appeared so by contrast with the barren country over which the wanderer had traveled; and this may be true, but it is not wise to analyze too severely the things that give us pleasure. They are few enough at best.

Our currency was the Mexican silver dollar, then at par, and the Mexican ounce, a gold coin worth sixteen dollars.

There were no banks, and no drafts or checks except those given out by the paymasters and quartermasters of the United States Army.

Everybody loaned money when he had it, but only for accommodation. I knew of only one man in the whole valley who loaned money at interest or required security.

It was no unusual thing for merchants to loan large quantities of their goods, bales of prints and muslin and sacks of sugar and coffee to their neighbor merchants, to be repaid in kind when their wagon train arrived.

Carriages and buggies were considered as almost community property, and the man who refused to lend them was considered a bad neighbor.

Everybody had credit at "the store," and everybody paid up—sooner or later.

There were no hotels. Travelers stopped at each other's houses and even strangers were welcome there. Any one having any claim to gentility or education was cheerfully received and entertained by the officers at the army posts, and many, *very many,* by the collector of customs at El Paso.

There was one peculiar fact about the El Paso of those early days, for which I could never give any good reason.

Perhaps there were several reasons.

Our little village was better known, or, rather, it had greater notoriety and elicited more interest and inquiry, than any other town in the United States of twenty times its population. I know this from my own experience during my visits to Eastern cities, and the same statement was made by every El Paso wanderer on returning home. I mean that a gentleman registering from El Paso in any of the great cities received more attention and was more questioned about his town than one from San Antonio or Denver.

It seemed impossible to go anywhere without meeting an army officer or some one who had lived at El Paso, or some stranger who had heard of the little hamlet and was eager to learn more.

In spite of privations, our little village seemed to have an unaccountable fascination for every one who saw it, refined American ladies as well as the less fastidious and sterner sex.

This was *my* El Paso. To me it was like the Deserted Village to Goldsmith.

The new El Paso got away from me. *Que sea por Dios.*

Our merchandise and supplies were brought from St. Louis, a distance of sixteen hundred miles, or from Port Lavaca, Texas, a distance of nine hundred miles, by large trains of immense freight wagons, "Schooners of the Plains," drawn by fourteen to eighteen mules, usually four abreast, at a cost of twelve and one-half to fifteen cents per pound for freight only. These trains were usually accompanied by twenty-five to forty men, including the drivers, all of whom were well armed, and stood guard like soldiers.

The "wagonmaster" was a character of importance and authority, and a hunter was usually employed to procure fresh meat and to look out for Indians and for Indian "sign." These trains, like the stage coaches, were often attacked by Indians, but because of the greater number of men and better means of defense, they were not so frequently "taken in" as the latter.

I quote here the prices of a few of the articles purchased by me of El Paso merchants during the "sixties," having preserved the original bills: One common No. 7 kitchen stove, $125; ham and bacon, 75 cents per pound; coffee, 75 cents per pound; sugar, 60 cents per pound; lard, 40 cents per pound; candles, 75 cents per pound; one-half ream letter paper, $4; nails, 50 cents per pound; matches, 12½ cents per box; tobacco, $2 per pound; calico (print), 50 cents per yard; bleached muslin, 75 cents per yard; unbleached muslin, 50 cents per yard; coal oil, $5 per gallon; alcohol, $8 per gallon; lumber, rough sawed, 12½ cents per foot; empty whiskey barrels, $5 each; starch, 50 cents per pound. But if we paid high prices, we also received high prices for what we had to sell. I will here state briefly a few of my own business experiences. I made large quantities of wine from the El Paso grape, and sold it readily at $5 per gallon, $200 per barrel of forty gallons. For two years I furnished the Government with all the vinegar and salt used in the Military Department of New Mexico, vinegar at $1.70 per gallon, and salt at 17 cents per pound, delivered at El Paso. Vinegar, four thousand gallons, and salt, one thousand bushels. The vinegar was manufactured from the El Paso grape, and the salt was brought from a natural salt lake, one hundred and twenty-five miles northeast of El Paso, and ground at Harts Mills, near El Paso, and sacked here.

The Government had previously been hauling these articles from St. Louis, a distance of sixteen hundred miles. My partner, Don Juan Zubiran, and myself one day delivered three hundred head of beef cattle to the Government at Las Cruces, New Mexico, at 18 cents per pound on the hoof—$90 per head. For a year I delivered beef on the block to the troops at Fort Bliss at 22 cents per pound.

I will now give some items from the other side of my ledger. Three hundred head of cattle belonging to my partner, Mr. Norboe, and myself were taken by Indians in Arizona in 1865, and half of our herders killed. These cattle were being driven to California, where there was then a good market. A white man, also a partner, got away with $11,000 worth of my cattle at Fort Sumner, New Mexico, by selling them and running away with the money.

Another partner, an honest man, died my debtor to the amount of $14,000. This would not have occurred had the gentleman not become insane and unable to settle his large and complicated business.

From the day of my first arrival at El Paso, I determined to make the place by permanent home, and I have never had any desire to change that choice. From the first I foresaw the prospective importance of the place, and many a still, lonesome night have I listened to the roaring of the waters over the dam at Harts Mill, a mile above the village, and tried to fancy it the rumbling of railroad trains, which were then fifteen hundred miles away. No, I do not claim to have foreseen that El Paso would be the center of so many railroads, but I felt sure that the first road to the Pacific Ocean would pass through El Paso, and *so it would,* had it not been for the Rebellion. I would not claim to have had this foresight, did not my letters to my friends during those early years (some of which are still extant) bear out the statement. I probably wrote more and spoke more about the certain future of El Paso than any one who ever lived here. I did more. I proved my faith by my acts. For ten years, amid all the folly and extravagance and vices of my bachelor youth, I kept one object constantly in view: to acquire and hold and pay taxes on a sufficient number of town lots to make me reasonably independent when the railroads should come, and for a time I owned more desirable property in El Paso than any other individual ever owned except the proprietors of the town tract.

Well, the greater portion of this valuable property was taken from me by corrupt courts and officials and by faithless lawyers and supposed friends, and by other means which I may or may not refer to in these writings. If any man says he would have defended himself and his rights better or more courageously than I did, I can only reply that I think I was fortunate to escape with my life! After all this, more than a hundred strangers (who never owned enough of mother earth to be buried in) have said to me: "You have been here a long time, Mr. Mills, and if you had only known what El Paso would be you could have bought town property very cheap and could have been wealthy," etc., etc. Then, for a moment, homicidal thoughts come into my mind. But it would do no good to kill such a man. A fool or two more or less in the world, or even in a community, would make no perceptible difference. There are so many!

It has been said these men of the frontier in those early days led indolent, idle lives in a "Sleepy Hollow," and that is true in a way.

The conditions were such that constant toil and endeavor were almost impossible. A train of wagons would arrive from Mexico with silver or other products and in a few days the El Paso merchant would sell or exchange thousands of dollars' worth of goods, and then for weeks he might not have a customer worthy of his attention.

Another man would labor almost incessantly night and day for a time in filling some Government contract, and then for months, perhaps, no other opportunity would offer for the exercise of his energy. It was "enforced idleness." But in the long run these men expended as much effort, physical and mental, in chasing the nimble dollar as the most plodding, methodical Chicago business man of today.

Profits were often great and risks were always great. I do not think the desire for money, for its own sake, was as strong as in older communities, and this led to what we called liberality and what the wise call extravagance. If any man had devoted all his energies to accumulating and hoarding money he would have been viewed with disfavor by his neighbors, and at that time men were in many ways dependent upon the good will of their fellows.

If any gentleman did not care to bet on the horse race or to "sit in" at the poker game, no one criticised his peculiarity, because each granted to the other the right he claimed for himself, to do as he pleased about such amusements. But if such a one gave out that he thus refrained because he feared to set a bad example to others or because he feared Divine wrath, his sincerity would have been doubted, and frankness and candor were rated among the essential virtues.

Within the memory of men still living there occurred an incident which illustrates men's views of law and order in those days. A certain desperado had been getting drunk and riding into stores and saloons and firing his pistols at random in the streets and threatening people's lives, till the "good citizens" became weary.

Finally he took a snap shot at the popular member of the Legislature, Mr. Jeff Hall, on the main street. This was too much. In a few moments fifteen or twenty of the aforesaid "good citizens" were chasing him over town with shotguns, rifles and pistols. The desperado was brought to earth in the corral of the old Central Hotel—"Hell's half acre"—pierced by many missiles. Then there was an animated dispute among the above-mentioned good citizens as to who had fired the fatal shot. One claimed to have done the work with his shotgun. Another said that such small ammunition at long range could not kill such a man, but that it was his rifle shot in the neck that did it. A third said that he had dispatched the deceased with three body shots from his sixshooter, and so on.

At last "Uncle Ben" Dowell said: "Gentlemen, some day some judge or other may come along and be holding court, and some of us may have trouble about this business." Thereupon they organized a coroner's jury, composed of the identical men who did the shooting, and sat upon the corpse and agreed upon a verdict, to the effect that "Deceased came to his death by gunshot wounds *from the hands of parties unknown.*"

It was about this time that an El Paso merchant, still living in this valley, had a little experience with the rough Americans here, mostly gamblers. There were many of the latter class.

At this time the fraternity were broke, and some of them had pawned their pistols with this merchant for money. But finally one of them reported to the "boys" that Mr. —— had refused to make any more loans on pistols. "How did you approach him?" was asked. "Why, I presented the handle of my pistol and asked him to loan me $25 on it." "Idiot," said "Snap"

Mitchell, the leader, "you don't know how to soak a pistol; watch me." So "Snap" went to the store and presenting the *muzzle* of his pistol asked for a loan. He got it, and went away with the pistol also.

I believe my friend remembers the transaction. Later this same merchant was called upon by a party of secessionists, who accused him of being a —— abolitionist, and talked to him seriously about the penalty, which was hanging. My friend was a foreigner and did not understand our language as well as he does now. I asked him what he said to them when they threatened to hang him, and he replied: "Well, I told them that I had no 'scruples.'" Of course, he meant that he had no preference for either the Union or Confederate cause. It is certain that he did not mean that he had no scruples about being hanged!

An officer of volunteers bought goods of this same merchant, refused to pay him, swindled him, and because asked to pay called him a —— Jew and other pet names, and finally sent him a formal challenge to fight a duel. The merchant came to me greatly agitated, and declared that he would rather die than suffer such indignities, and asked my advice. I knew that he was in earnest, and the officer was notified to appear at sunrise at the graveyard on the hill, distance ten paces, double-barreled shotguns loaded with buckshot, to fire at the word. The officer declined, declaring the terms "barbarous," and that ended his career as a valiant son of Mars.

MURDER AND ROBBERY OF GIDDINGS' STORE (SHELDON BLOCK).

In 1859 the San Antonio Mail Company had its headquarters on the lot where the Sheldon building now stands. They had in the old adobe house as large a stock of general merchandise as any El Paso merchant now carries. The clerks who slept in the store were a Mr. Atkins, familiarly known as "Ole Dad," and "Fred" ——, a young German. One night Atkins was absent and Fred was sleeping in the store alone.

The next morning a window in the south side of the building was found to have been dug out of the wall and poor Fred was lying dead in his bed with fourteen knife wounds in his body. A large amount of money had been taken from the store (there were no safes nor banks here then) and quantities of valuable goods had also been carried away. This was evidently the work of robbers from the Mexican side of the river. No trace of the robbers or money or goods was ever discovered.

After this murder Mr. Atkins declined to sleep in the store alone. The writer was at that time clerking for St. Vrain & Co., merchants, in the old Central Hotel building, which was burned down a few years ago. As we had plenty of people to protect the St. Vrains store it was agreed that I should go over each night and sleep in the store which had been robbed. But soon the scare was over and Atkins, saying that "lightning never struck twice in the same place," left me alone for one night. I had a shotgun and pistol, and a good watchdog. The merchants of the village had employed a Mr. Cullimore (now of Austin, Tex.), familiarly called "Bones," to patrol the town of nights.

That night about 2 o'clock I heard the report of both barrels of "Bones'" shotgun resounding in the little plaza, and his voice calling to me to "look out, Mills!" Robbers, probably the same party, had commenced to dig out the same window and had half finished the work when "Bones" fired on them without effect. They fled, of course, and left only a hat and handkerchief on the ground as remembrances. It was long before any one would sleep alone in that store.

THE CANBY-SIBLEY CAMPAIGN IN 1861-2.

The following notes are published substantially as they were written soon after the close of the campaign. The remoteness of New Mexico from the scenes of vastly more important conflicts prevented historians of the war from writing of that campaign, which, though insignificant by comparison, was one of the knightliest and most romantic in history. I have here aimed to do justice to the brave men, of both armies, who marched and countermarched, and fought and fled and fought again along the banks of the Rio Grande forty years ago.

In 1858, when still a youth, accident and adventure brought me to El Paso. * * * Determining to make my home in this valley, and being without money or friends or a profession, I commenced life as a merchant's clerk. I had spent about three years in that capacity when the news of the firing on Fort Sumter and the inglorious surrender by General Twiggs, of all the United States troops in Texas, startled us as much, though ten days old, as though the lightning had brought it. We had heard a great deal of street corner talk about secession, and a packed convention had passed a resolution declaring Texas out of the Union, which resolution had been submitted to a vote of the people; my brother (now Col. Anson Mills), myself and only two or three others voting against it in El Paso County. The Mexican voters, of course, knew but little about the questions involved in secession and were influenced by the Americans, most of whom favored se-

*"All of which I saw and a part of which I was."

cession, those of Northern birth being loudest in their protestations of devotion to the South and loudest in denunciation of "abolitionists," which meant all who did not favor rebellion.

There was at that time a garrison of United States troops at Fort Bliss, within a mile of El Paso; another at Fort Quitman, ninety miles below, on the river, and several other posts in striking distance, all of which were included in the surrender of General Twiggs to the "Texas commissioners" at San Antonio, 700 miles away! There was not a Confederate soldier within 500 miles of Fort Bliss, but such is the power of military discipline that the post commander, Colonel Reives, though urged by my brother and myself and others to disregard Twiggs' order of surrender, turned over his arms and valuable stores to Commissioner McGoffin and marched with his command, as prisoners, to San Antonio.

Then we determined that my brother should go to Washington city and report the condition of affairs here, and try to get the Secretary of War to order these officers not to respect Twiggs' surrender, but he arrived too late.

I and a younger brother, Emmet Mills, remained at El Paso. The feeling against Union men grew still more bitter. I could see no good in rebellion. I was willing to make some sacrifices and incur some dangers for my flag and country.

Colonel Loring at that time commanded the United States troops in the adjoining territory of New Mexico. There was a garrison at Fort Fillmore, fifty miles north of El Paso, but United States officers who had resigned (?) and passed through El Paso going south, gave out that Loring was "with the South."

By this time a small force of Texas troops were en route to El Paso and New Mexico and it was claimed that Fort Fillmore would be surrendered without a fight.

I then went to Fort Fillmore and en route was given a letter, with the request that I was to hand it to Captain Lane, then commanding that post. Being introduced to Captain Lane, in conversation about secession he complained that we El Paso people had taken advantage of his position to treat him badly. He said we knew his feelings were with the South, and that we had presumed upon the fact in taking his horses and placing him in an embarrassing position. He said he could recapture the horses and destroy our town, but he would not. This satisfied me that nothing could be hoped for from him. Of course, Lane supposed that I was in sympathy with rebellion, and for good reasons I did not undeceive him. I told him in a jocular way that he might as well turn over his saddles as they were useless to him without horses, at which he became angry and I left him. I then proceeded to the town of La Messilla, five miles from the fort, and found a secession flag flying in the street and the secession leaders notifying Union men to leave. They had held a convention and organized a Confederate territorial government for what they called Arizona.

By this time Colonel Loring had passed south to join the Confederates. Gen. E. R. S. Canby was now in command of the Department of New Mexico, with headquarters at Santa Fe. From Messilla I wrote to Hon. John S. Watts at Santa Fe as follows:

"La Messilla, N. M., June 23, 1861.

"Hon. John S. Watts: Sir—I came up here from El Paso two days ago hoping to meet you. I assure you that I found matters here in a deplorable condition. A disunion flag is now flying from the house in which I write, and this country is now as much in the possession of the enemy as Charleston is. All the officers at Fort Fillmore except two, are devotedly with the South, and are only holding on to their commissions in order to embarrass our Government and at the proper time to turn over everything to the South, after the manner of General Twiggs. The Messilla Times is bitterly disunion and threatens with death any one who refuses to acknowledge this usurpation. There is, however, a latent Union sentiment, especially among the Mexicans, but they are effectually overawed. * * * The regular soldiers, in defiance of the teachings of their officers and the offer of gold from Hart, are yet faithful, and if a second lieutenant were to ask them to follow him they would tear down the secession flag and throw the Times office into the river in an hour. Fifty of them could go to Fort Bliss and capture all the Government stores at that place, but instead of this a few thieves came up from El Paso and stole forty of the horses belonging to a mounted company at Fort Fillmore. No effort was made to recapture these horses, although the soldiers plead with their officers to allow them to do so. * * * About 300 Texans are expected at Fort Bliss in about two weeks, and if something is not done before that time Fort Fillmore will be surrendered. Very respectfully, W. W. Mills."

(The above letter is copied from the Records of the Rebellion.)

In contrast with this letter, and to show the plots and counterplots of those days, I copy from the same page of the Rebellion Records the following:

"Hart's Mills, Tex., June 12, 1861.

"Col. W. W. Loring: We are at last under the glorious banner of the Confederate States of America. * * * We shall have no trouble in reaching San Antonio. Four companies of Texas troops have been ordered to garrison this post (Fort Bliss). Meanwhile Colonel Magoffin, Judge Hart and Crosby are very much exercised and concerned on account of the public stores here in their present unguarded condition. Meanwhile, you may, by delaying your departure (from New Mexico) a week or two, add much to the security of this property.

"I regret now, more than ever, the sickly sentimentality by which I was overruled in my desire of bringing my whole command with me from New Mexico. I wish I had my part to play over again*

"Should you be relieved of your command too soon to prevent an attempt on the part of your successor to recapture the property here send a notice by extraordinary express to Judge Hart. Your seat in the stage to San Antonio may be engaged. * * * Faithfully yours, H. H. Sibley."

(Note.—Sibley, who afterward commanded the Texas expedition, was a major of United States cavalry and Colonel Loring was then commanding, and betraying, the United States troops in New Mexico.)

Judge Watts indorsed my letter to General Canby, who sent a young officer, Lieutenant Hall, to Fort Fillmore with a copy of it, to investigate and report. * * * General Canby read Major Sibley's letter of June 12th and mine of June 23d on June 29th, and Major Lynde having assumed command of Fort Fillmore he (Canby) wrote that officer as follows:

*Did Arnold experience similar regrets and wishes?

"Headquarters Department of New Mexico,
"Santa Fe, N. M., June 30, 1861.

"Maj. I. Lynde, Seventh Inf., Comdg. Fort Fillmore, N. M.: Sir—I had occasion on the 24th inst. to put you on your guard against the alleged complicity of Colonel Loring in the treasonable designs of the Texas authorities at Fort Bliss and El Paso. I now send a copy of one and extracts from another letter sent to me after the arrival of the mail yesterday, which fully confirm all the information I had previously received. Although Colonel Loring was still in the department, I have not hesitated, since this information was communicated to me, to exercise the command and to give any orders or to take any measures that I considered necessary to protect the honor or the interests of the Government.

"Sibley's letter shows the Texas authorities at Fort Bliss and El Paso count upon Colonel Loring's aid in furthering their plans and indicates the manner (by delaying his departure) in which this aid is to be rendered. Colonel Loring's resignation was tendered on the 13th of last month, and has doubtless long since been accepted; but this is not material, for any failure to act at once, or any hesitancy in acting, may be in the highest degree disastrous. In this case, then, as in all similar cases which may occur, you will at once arrest the implicated parties and hold them securely until their guilt or innocence can be determined by the proper tribunals. No considerations of delicacy or of regard must be permitted to interfere when the honor of the country and the safety of your command are involved. I send these communications by Lieutenant Hall, Tenth Infantry. Very respectfully, sir, your obedient servant,

"Ed. R. S. Canby,
"Brevet Lieutenant-Colonel, U. S. Army, Comdg. Dept."

I then returned to El Paso and settled my affairs preparatory to going to Santa Fe to take part with the Union people. There was then residing at El Paso a Col. Phil Herbert, who had been a member of Congress from California, but who, on account of bad conduct or misfortune, had left the State under a cloud. Having never seen anything in the conduct of this gentleman that was not honorable, generous and brave, it is not for me to speak of his supposed faults. He was an enthusiastic rebel, but my personal friend. When the stage coach was ready to start I took this man aside and confided to him where I was going, and why I was going. He approved of my determination and wished me personal success. I passed Fort Fillmore again en route to Santa Fe, July 1, 1861, and met Dr. Cooper McKee, the post surgeon, whom I knew well, and appealed to him to do something to prevent the surrender of the post. He appeared displeased at my remarks about his brother officers, and said that their sympathies or intentions were not his business, nor mine.

I met at the post another young army surgeon, Dr. Alden, who had lately arrived from Santa Fe. I found him as enthusiastic and as distrustful of the officers as myself. He told me he had thought of sending a private express to General Canby, advising him of the danger, but as I was going he would intrust it to me. He promised to meet me next day in Mesilla, and did so, but such was the feeling against Union men that this United States officer, almost under the guns of his post, did not dare to speak to me on the street, but beckoned me to an outhouse, where he privately handed me a letter to Lieutenant Anderson, Canby's adjutant.

I then called upon Dr. M. Steck, a loyal man, who was Indian agent, and received from him some encouragement and a letter to some friends of the government at Santa Fe. We started the next morning to Santa Fe by stage coach. There were nine passengers, all Union men, I believe, and well armed. When about ten miles out we were overtaken by a Mexican courier with a note for Don Lorena Labide, a loyal Mexican passenger, informing him that a force of rebel horsemen had left Mesilla that morning, intending to capture the stage at the Point of Rocks that night. We held a consultation and determined to proceed and fight if attacked. When near the Point of Rocks eight of us got off the coach, with arms, and followed it at a distance, instructing the driver that if halted he should get them into a parley and give us the first fire. We, however, passed the point unmolested, probably because a company of United States troops camped near there. I went into this camp and found Lieutenant McNalley, with his company, en route to Fort Fillmore, and informed him of the condition of affairs there. At my request he gave us an escort. I found him loyal and ready for any duty. Arriving at Santa Fe I was introduced to General Canby, and delivered Dr. Alden's letter to his adjutant, Captain Anderson, who read it and handed it to Canby.

I made a verbal report of all I had seen and heard. General Canby informed me that he would order Captain Lane away from Fort Fillmore, and he did. The general also stated that he had ordered Maj. Isaac Lynde to leave his station in Arizona and take command of Fillmore. He had confidence in Lynde, and, telling me something of his plans, requested me to return to Fort Fillmore with dispatches for that officer.

I arrived at Las Cruces, six miles from Fillmore, with these dispatches at sunset about the 15th of July, and met Dr. Steck, who avoided recognizing me. I took a room in the hotel, locked the door and tried to sleep. About 10 o'clock Dr. Steck came by stealth to my room to advise me of danger. The contents of my letter to Canby had been unwisely made known, and even United States officers were threatening vengeance.

Before reaching the fort next morning I met two loyal friends, Dr. Knour, now of Las Vegas, and Mr. Brady, who also informed me that I had been threatened. I rode into the post and met Captain Lane, who angrily asked me if I had reported him to General Canby as a traitor. I replied that I had stated facts and left General Canby to draw his own conclusions. A strange officer then asked if I had said or written anything about him. He said whoever called him a traitor was a liar. That night he ran away from the post and joined the rebels at Bliss. This was one Captain Garland.

I called on Major Lynde and delivered my dispatches. He sent for his adjutant, Lieutenant Brooks, who opened and read them with some remarks, which satisfied me that he was not anxious to lose much blood in defense of his country. I believe, though I cannot know, that a message went that night to Colonel Baylor, who had arrived at Fort Bliss with his command, informing him of the contents of these dispatches. There was an order from Canby to Lynde to recapture Fort Bliss and the stores there, which he could easily have done.

After Brooks withdrew Lynde spoke to me of the feeling among his officers against me. He said he believed I had acted honestly, but unwisely. Many of his officers, he said, sympathized with the South, but they had pledged their honors that, as long as they remained in the service they would stand my him. I pleaded, entreated and tried to reason with him for half an hour. I told him treachery and ruin were all around him. "He had six hundred regular troops, well armed and eager for the fray." I advised him to arrest a few officers and send them under guard to Canby! To march on Fort Bliss and capture the three hundred half-armed Texans and the military stores which had been surrendered there. Poor old man! It was useless. I have never seen Lynde since that day, but ten years later I received a letter, from which I extract the following:

"St. Paul, October 22, 1871.

"W. W. Mills: Dear Sir—Well do I remember the interview you refer to, but I did not believe then that my junior officers would act toward me as they did. Sincerely yours, I. Lynde."

Major Lynde, in answer to Canby's letter indorsing me insisted that I should undertake to learn and report the exact strength of Colonel Baylor's command, promising to fight him if it was not stronger than represented. I consented to undertake this dangerous service, but before starting I went to Dr. McKee's quarters. Several officers were there. The doctor received me by saying that he had been my friend, but I had incurred the displeasure of his brother officers and he could be so no longer. Doctor Alden said I had misrepresented him, that he had never doubted the loyalty or good faith of any officer. I reminded him of his letter to Anderson. He replied that it was only a friendly letter, having no reference to military matters.

A year later, when in the field with Captain Anderson, he referred to his files and found Alden's letter to be a warning of treachery and danger. The gallant Lieutenant McNalley was present, but appeared to be in doubt. I have never seen him since, but subsequent events must have satisfied him of the truth of my representations to him that night on the Jornado del Muerto.

But I am running ahead of my story. I procured a horse from my friend, Dr. Knour, and rode to Paso del Norte (Jaurez, Mexico), fifty miles in six hours, to watch Colonel Baylor, keeping off the road. While en route, at Canntilla, I met a deserter from Baylor's command, Sergeant Kemp, whom I knew to be a Union man who had been forced by circumstances to join the Texans. I gave him a letter of credence to Major Lynde, and he reported the exact strength of Baylor's command, but Lynde moved not. Several efforts were made to decoy me off the streets of Juarez, so as to kidnap me, but I saw through the design and avoided them.

One morning I met three acquaintances near the bridge on the main street, and as I had a letter for one of them I saluted them with "Good morning, gentlemen." One of them, Kelly, secession editor of the Mesilla newspaper, said: "So you are a spy." I replied: "No, who says I am?" He said: "I do." "Then you are a liar." He struck at me, but I avoided the blow and placed a cocked pistol at his breast. He threw up his arms and said, "Don't fire," and I put up my pistol. Kelly was soon after killed by Colonel Baylor in a street fight at Mesilla. (Kelly was from Michigan.) There was at that time, at El Paso, a German named Kuhn, whom I knew, and who had the reputation of being a bad man. He professed to hate the Texans, and I did not suspect him of any connection with them.

I was ready to return to New Mexico when one day about noon, when walking on the sidewalk near the corner of the plaza in front of the store of Mr. Duchene, I saw that Dutchman Kuhn on horseback in front of me, apparently drunk. I wished to avoid him, but as

I neared him he rode onto the sidewalk and seized me by the shoulder. Half a dozen other horsemen appeared, as though they had risen out of the ground. One seized my pistol and ordered me to mount his horse quickly. I did so, and he vaulted up behind me, and away we all went a clattering gallop toward the Texas side. When we had crossed the river I asked, "Where do you intend to take me?" One answered, "To Fort Bliss." I requested that they would not take me through El Paso, but they decided to do so. Kuhn then said to me that it was all right, I would have a fair trial and so on. I said: "I want no talk with you, sir; you are a scoundrel and a murderer. These soldiers obey orders. You betray for money." I said more, and offered to fight him if they would give me my pistol. As I expected, this piece of pluck won the chivalrous young Texans. I saw no possibility of escape, and knowing the bitter feeling against me it appeared to me the chances were in favor of being hung or shot. Not that I considered myself a spy, for I had not been in disguise nor in the enemy's lines, but I did not suppose those gentlemen would hesitate much about technicalities.

To a soldier taken in battle imprisonment merely means exchange or parole, but this was a different matter. It was not probable that the soil of a neutral republic had been violated merely that the Texan officers might have the pleasure of my company about their quarters. At Fort Bliss I was taken before the then post commander, Major Waller, who said: "You are brought here a prisoner, sir." I asked why they had taken me from neutral soil, and he said I would learn in time. He then sent for the officer of the day, Capt. Ike Stafford, who conducted me to the guardhouse; it was filled with vermin and bad men. (Captain Stafford still lives in Texas.)

The first night a blacksmith came and took the measure of my ankle, and presently returned with a ball and chain which he rivetted on my leg. I soon found that by removing my boot I could slip the iron over my foot, but the chances for escape were very poor, and I often shuddered when awakened from troubled sleep by its clanking. The idea of kidnaping me did not originate with the Texan military, but was instigated by citizen non-combatants—my own neighbors.

The next day two of the young men who kidnaped me came to see me at the guard house. Their names were Craig and McGarvey—James McGarvey, now of Galveston. Before they left they promised to be my friends, and faithfully kept their words. They told me that Kuhn had offered to divide with them the reward paid him for my arrest, but they declined the blood-money.

Colonel Herbert also called to see me, and denounced my arrest and volunteered to act as my counsel.

The colonel applied for a writ of habeas corpus, but the district judge refused to grant it.

I asked to see Colonel Baylor, and asked to be tried and hung or shot or released. He said he had evidence enough to hang me, though he would dislike to do it. Still, if I insisted, he would give me a court martial. He recounted very correctly some of the incidents of my journey to Santa Fe.

The next day Baylor sent his adjutant to inform me that he could not grant a court martial.

Before my arrest I had written my brother Emmitt, who was employed on the overland stage line west of Mesilla, that there would be fighting between the Texas and United States troops, and suggested that he come in and report to the commanding officer at Fort Fillmore.

He came, but received no encouragement at Fillmore, and learning of my arrest and being in danger of rebels at Mesilla, he attempted to make his way toward California. He went in the mail coach with a party of six other young men, all well armed.

At Cook's canyon, about one hundred miles west of Mesilla, they were attacked by a large body of Apache Indians under Mangas Coloradas, "Bloody Sleeves," and one of the most desperate frontier fights on record ensued. It appears that our friends had time to gain the top of a little hill and build a stone breastwork about two feet high, inclosing a space about twelve feet square. A freighter, Mr. Deguere, who passed the scene a few days later with his wagons, found and buried the bodies and found everywhere the evidences of a terrible struggle. Under a stone, on the top of the wall, he found a pencil note, dated July 23d, 1861, stating that they had been fighting two days; had killed many Indians; that all were now killed or wounded except two; that they were out of water and would try to escape that night. I have visited the scene of this conflict. A tree, not more than ten inches in diameter, about one hundred yards from the fortification, has many marks of bullets evidently discharged from inside the wall. I give a list of the names of these brave men, the extent of whose daring and suffering can never be known in this strange life of ours. They were: Emmett Mills, Freeman Thomas, Joe Roacher, M. Champion, John Pontel, Bob Avlin and John Wilson. *All were killed.* The Indians who sold their arms and watches in Mexico said that they lost forty warriors in the fight. The newspaper containing this sad account was thrown to me through the window of my prison.

It was about this time that I stood at the door of the

guard house and saw Colonel Baylor with less than three hundred poorly armed Texans start on his march to capture Fort Fillmore, then garrisoned by seven hundred and fifty regular troops, the flower of the United States army, and I knew and said that he would succeed. That history is a short one. Baylor took possession of the town of Mesilla unopposed, Major Lynde made a show of attempting to dislodge him, and a skirmish ensued in which Lieutenant McNally, not yet knowing that it was only mimic war, exposed himself and was wounded.

Lynde retreated in good order(?) and that night abandoned the post and fled in the direction of Fort Stanton. A show was made of destroying the stores at the post, but very little damage was done. All was confusion and demoralization. A patriotic quartermaster, Lieutenant Plummer, left some government drafts in his pockets at his quarters. These were sent to Washington indirectly by the rebels, and the money collected.

The command marched, or straggled, to San Augustine Springs, eighteen miles east of Fillmore, where being overtaken by Colonel Baylor with about two hundred men, they surrendered unconditionally without firing a gun. No sooner was the surrender an accomplished fact than the same subordinate officers who had aided to bring it about, some by indifference, some by sympathy and some by treachery, united in charging the whole responsibility upon poor old Lynde.

Major Lynde was dismissed from the service, but was reinstated after the war. He was not treacherous, he was weak, and he was deceived to his ruin and the disgrace of his flag. I have never doubted but that had he been properly supported and encouraged the result would have been different. Of his subalterns some resigned, some joined the enemy and some went into the recruiting and quartermaster's service, none, so far as I know, except McNally ever did much fighting. I do not censure all of them, but I thought, and still think, that there should have been one among them who would have assumed command, arrested Lynde, and won a colonel's eagles.

When Colonel Baylor returned to Fort Bliss he sent to me and proposed to release me on parole. I refused to give my parole, and he informed me that I was released from close confinement and given the limits of the post. "But," said he, "if you attempt to escape to the enemy's lines I will capture and hang you."

The secret of my release was that General Canby had arrested at Santa Fe a prominent secessionist, General Pelham, and, placing him in prison, threatened him with the same treatment that I should receive, and Canby was a man of his word.

At the request of my friends, McGarvey, Craig and others, the "limits of the post" were enlarged as to me, so that finally I drifted to the Mexican side of the river. I had been confined about thirty days, in July and August, 1861.

The nearest United States troops were at Fort Craig, one hundred and seventy-five miles north of El Paso, but I determined to make the journey. I obtained a horse from Craig and bought another, and secured the services of a Mexican who claimed to be a guide.

We started at 11 p. m. from Juarez. We crossed the river below Concordia and traveled north on the east side of the Organ Mountains, avoiding all roads. When we thought we had reached a point nearly east of Fort Craig, we rode west across the mountains. The journey was not so easy as I supposed. The guide did not know the country, and, the weather being cloudy, we were lost in the mountains. When the sun came out we traveled west, knowing that we must strike the river somewhere. The fifth morning out from El Paso we heard the band play guard mount at Fort Craig, and rising a little hill my heart was gladdened by the sight of the flag of my country.

This post, Fort Craig, was then commanded by Col. B. S. Roberts, of the regular army, a brave and true soldier, who was concentrating a force to resist General Sibley, who was then (December, 1861) en route from San Antonio with a force of thirty-five hundred Texans to capture and hold New Mexico. Colonel Roberts received me very kindly, and after I had made a written report of what I had seen and learned, offered to procure me a captain's commission in the New Mexican volunteers (Kit Carson's regiment) or to get me a commission as first lieutenant and place me on his staff as aide-de-camp. I chose the latter.

Early in February, 1862, General Sibley arrived before Fort Craig with his whole force and a battery of six guns, Major Teel's. Roberts had collected, to oppose him, one thousand regulars, two regiments of Mexican volunteers (natives), under Colonels Carson and Peno, and two companies of Colorado volunteers. Two companies of our infantry had been detached and trained to a battery of six guns, under the brave, unfortunate Captain McRae. On a Sunday evening the Texans appeared in force in front of the post, and we marched out to fight them in the plain, but they retired.

That night they crossed to the east bank of the Rio Grande, below Fort Craig, and next morning commenced to pass round the post by a road which our engineers had declared impassable. Their advance reached the river five miles above the post at 9 o'clock a. m. at Valverde, since changed to San Marcial. General Canby, who had arrived at Fort Craig, ordered Colonel Roberts to check them with the cavalry, and I went with him. We drove their advance back from the water, and Roberts sent me back to report to General Canby that the enemy's whole force would reach the river before noon, and to ask for re-enforcements. Canby sent Major Selden's column of infantry, six hundred strong, McRae's battery, Carson's New Mexico volunteers and the two Colorado companies.

When we reached the scene of action the enemy had arrived at the foot of the hills, about a mile east of the river, there being between them and the river a level plain studded here and there with cottonwood trees, but in places the ground was open. Our right and their left rested on a round mountain on the east bank of the river. This was February 21st, 1862.

THE BATTLE OF VALVERDE.

This peaceful valley, which had scarcely before echoed to the report of the sportsman's fowling piece, was now to resound to the thunders of artillery and become the scene of bloody conflict. The west bank of the river where we first took position, was an open, level plain. The Texans had advanced their battery and support into a clump of trees about three hundred yards from the bank of the river and almost in the shadow of the mountain. They were in position when McRae arrived. McRae unlimbered on the very brink of the river, and this fierce artillery duel commenced. It did not last more than thirty minutes.

Though McRae's loss was heavy, his victory was complete. Teel's battery was rendered useless for that day. When the artillery fight was nearly over Roberts sent me across the river with an order to Capt. David H. Brotherton to charge the enemy's battery with his two companies of infantry, and to bring Major Duncan's cavalry to his support. Brotherton prepared to obey promptly, but as Duncan refused to obey the order I took the responsibility of recalling Brotherton and was commended for so doing. The enemy had now advanced toward the river in force, and Roberts ordered Selden with his infantry to cross the river, advance into the wood and attack with the bayonet if necessary. The men received the order with a shout and plunged into the river, which was cold and reached up to their armpits. Right gallantly did they obey the order, but they encountered double their number, strongly posted, and were compelled to retire, which they did in good order. Meantime our two Colorado companies had done good service on our left. They were dressed in gray like our militia, and the Texans, mistaking them for Mexicans, charged them recklessly. The Colorado men reserved their fire for close quarters, and emptied many saddles at the first fire. The remainder retired in disorder.

The New Mexican volunteers were keeping the enemy from the water and skirmishing briskly at times. There was now, at 2 o'clock p. m., a lull in the fighting. Some of us had lunch and talked of the prospects. So far all was favorable to us except the repulse of Selden.

We had kept them from the water, McRae had beaten their battery, and the Coloradans had gained an advantage. We were well posted and provided; their animals and men were weary and without water—they could not retreat; they must surrender or starve or fight quickly and desperately. During this lull Roberts crossed our battery to the east bank and placed Selden in support of it.

At 3 o'clock that afternoon General Canby appeared on the field and was received with cheers by the troops. After a brief consultation with Roberts he advanced our battery about five hundred yards, withdrew Selden from its support, leaving only two companies to protect it, and opened fire. Carson's Mexican regiment had been moved to our right and advanced, and with one company of regulars repulsed a charge of Texas cavalry with some loss. I observed Carson closely. He walked up and down his line, quietly encouraging his men with such words as "Firme, muchachos, firme" (steady, boys, be firm).

The Texans now rapidly concentrated all their available force at the foot of the hills in front of our battery for one last desperate charge. On they came, on foot, a mass of wild men, without order and apparently without command, with rifles, shotguns, pistols and all kinds of arms, and yelling like demons. Colonel Roberts saw the danger and ordered me to bring all the strength possible to charge their flank as they neared the battery. I found Major Duncan with his cavalry in an advantageous position, and gave him the order, but again he failed to obey. Turning to Captain Wingate, with his two companies of infantry, he responded promptly and was immediately on the jump. But he was soon mortally wounded, and Stone, his second officer, being killed, the movement was checked.

I returned to the battery. The small support was giving away; Canby, whose horse had been shot, was on foot. He had taken a musket from a retreating soldier and was urging the men to re-form and charge. It was too late. The battery worked on to the last moment. Captain McRae and his first lieutenant, Michler, were killed at their guns. Bell, the second lieutenant, was wounded. Of the ninety-three men belonging to the battery less than forty escaped. The contest was now ended, but notwithstanding this disaster, we retired to the post "with the regularity of a dress parade."

Considering the numbers actually engaged, Valverde was one of the best fought and one of the most sanguinary conflicts of the war, the mortality on either side being near one hundred. Five officers of the regular army, McRae, Michler, Wingate, Stone and Bascom, were killed in that fight. I admired General Canby (since treacherously murdered by the Modocs) alike for his courage as for his amiable character, but I believe that if Colonel Roberts had been left to carry out his plans that day Valverde would have been a Union victory and the campaign closed. General Sibley, although present, did not seem to develop during the day. The fighting was done mostly by Green, Scurry, Lockridge and Pryon. The day after the battle a flag of truce was borne into the post by Colonel Scurry, Major Ochiltre and another. Scurry being an acquaintance inquired for me, and I was present at the interview. They demanded a surrender of the post, which Canby of course refused. Some time was spent in refreshment and conversation, and they retired.

To condense and conclude this story, the Texans reconsidered their threat of taking Fort Craig and took up their march for Santa Fe. We followed, leaving a sufficient garrison in the post, but it was not Canby's intention to bring on a decisive engagement. He had other plans.

The Texans took possession of Santa Fe, the capital of the Territory, without opposition; but their good fortune allured them too far. They determined to attempt the capture of the Government supply depot, Fort Union, east of Santa Fe. Colonel Scurry commanded this expedition. At Pidgon's ranch (Glorietta) they met Colonel Slough's command of Colorado volunteers, and the regulars from Fort Union under Colonel Paul, who had united. Another battle took place almost as desperate and fatal as Valverde. In numbers they were about equal, but the result was favorable to the Federals, chiefly because during the day a detachment was sent to the Texan's rear, which under the direction and lead of Colonel Collins, a brave citizen, utterly destroyed their supply train. They slept hungry that night and then retreated in haste to Santa Fe. Meantime Canby had from Albuquerque opened communication with Paul and Slough, and a junction was effected at Tejaras, thirty miles east of Albuquerque.

Sibley had now commenced his retreat to Texas. Our combined forces under Canby by a silent forced march overtook them at 2 o'clock one morning at Peralto, the home of the loyal Governor Connolly. We camped within two miles of Peralto without being discovered. We could hear the sounds of revelry at the governor's house, then Sibley's headquarters. A brief consultation was held. Roberts proposed to "go in at daybreak and wake them up with the bayonet," and, of course, the whole command would have voted to do so but Canby's policy was to drive them out of the county without further loss of life—to "win a victory without losing men," he said, and perhaps he was wise.

We skirmished all that day, with advantages in our favor, but neither commander seemed disposed to bring on a general engagement, and that night Sibley, with the full knowledge of Canby, continued his retreat down the Rio Grande, a portion of our troops following them as far as El Paso.

Of the thirty-five hundred Texans who entered New Mexico only about eleven hundred returned to Texas. The others were dead, wounded, sick, prisoners or deserters. Many were buried on the west side of El Paso street, near where the Opera House now stands.

This was a disastrous expedition. They were brave men, but their management, discipline and at times their food, was not good, and the mortality from disease was great.

I accompanied Colonel Roberts to Santa Fe, where he detailed me as post quartermaster, but learning that, while I was a prisoner at Fort Bliss President Lincoln had appointed me collector of customs at El Paso, and not intending to follow the profession of arms, I resigned and returning to the home from which I had been driven, took possession of that office.

CAPTAIN MOORE.

While serving at Fort Craig, as above related, and when the Texans were advancing from El Paso nearer to Fort Craig, we had an outpost of two companies at a village called Alamosa, thirty miles south of Craig, on the Rio Grande, under command of Capt. —— Moore of the United States cavalry. One morning General Roberts said to me: "Take an escort and go and see what is going on at Alamosa." That was all the order I had. I went and met the younger officers, who told me that their captain was "in a bad way" and had been for several days. Going to Captain Moore's quarters I found him in a hopeless state of intoxication. After interrogating him until I was thoroughly satisfied of his condition, I demanded his sword and ordered him to go with my escort and report to General Roberts in arrest.

I charged the sergeant to take good care of him but did not think of his pistol. When they arrived in view of Fort Craig Captain Moore drew his pistol and *blew out his own brains!"*

Captain Moore had the reputation of being a good officer, with only that one fault, and of course the tragedy, and my connection with it made me sad—but what else could I have done? My action was approved and commended.

After this campaign General Roberts, being in Washington and testifying before the Congressional Committee on the conduct of the war, said: "One young man, W. W. Mills, who had the courage to stand up at El

Paso and Fort Bliss against the secessionists, was thrown into prison there and kept in confinement and in irons for a long time and his life threatened. He succeeded in making his escape and in reaching Fort Craig, having undergone great hardship, being three days without anything to eat and without water.

"Because of his loyalty and services General Canby appointed him an acting lieutenant. He was my aide-de-camp at the battle of Valverde, and his conduct there was not only meritorious, it was highly distinguished for zeal, daring and efficiency."—(Report of Committee, part 3d, page 271.)

I believe every young American of spirit has a natural desire for some romantic adventure requiring unusual exertion and involving some danger. I possessed this desire and it was fully gratified. That the Confederate soldiers manifested magnificent courage and devotion I freely grant. They once preserved my life from what General Scott termed "the fury of the non-combatants;" but I am glad that my feeble efforts were put forth in behalf of a cause which the civilized world has approved and the righteousness of which no one now questions, I believe. I have met many bitter partisans in my time, but I have never heard any one attempt to defend or excuse the actions of Twiggs or Loring or Sibley or Garland or any of the officers who connived at or assisted in and about the disgraceful surrender of Major Lynde as related in these pages. Few young men ever came home from the perils of camp, prison and battlefield more victorious or better vindicated than did the writer to El Paso with the Federal forces in 1862.

The very *charge* against me then was that I had been the leader of the Union people of this frontier.

While the advocates of secession had been more active and boisterous in their display of power than the friends of the Government had been, there was a strong latent Union sentiment even among the Americans, and with the Mexicans it was universal; so that a large majority approved of my course and rejoiced at my safe return.

Some who had bitterly opposed and even wronged me came to make peace (and promises), and I repulsed no man, because I felt that I could afford to be generous and desired to live in peace with my neighbors.

There were a few who still cherished the hope and belief that the Confederate cause would ultimately succeed, and that the El Paso Valley would be recaptured, and I would fare even worse than before; and the very few of these latter who are yet living, while they do not now, as then, denounce me as a "Union man" or as being "false to my home and fireside," still occasionally intimate that I must have been guilty of *something* wrong—but they do not specify what the wrong was.

I organized the Republican party in El Paso County, and for a decade I controlled its politics. Yes; a political "boss," if you will have it so, but I never purchased any votes nor juggled any man out of an election after he had won it, as was done in the case of Adolph Krakaner after he had been fairly and honestly elected Mayor of El Paso in April, 1889.

A STORY WITHOUT A MORAL.

On my return journey from Washington City in 1863, when traveling in the stage coach with driver and two other passengers, we halted for supper and a change of animals at a village seventy miles north of Fort Craig, where, falling in with some officers who had served with me during the then recent campaign, I accompanied them to their tents and there became so interested in telling and hearing stories that I forgot all about time and the stage went forward without me. I was the more to blame for this thoughtlessness because I was at the time bearing important official dispatches.

With many regrets and self-reproaches and good resolutions for the future, I procured a Government horse and started alone for Fort Craig, riding all night. I arrived at Fort Craig in due time safe and well, but learned that the stage coach had been attacked by Indians and that the driver and two passengers had been killed. It is certainly right to teach schoolboys (as I did forty years ago) that promptness, perseverance, diligence and watchfulness will greatly increase their chances for success, but is it right to teach them that by these means or by any other means they can *command* success? But I am not writing moral philosophy or solving riddles.

BENJAMIN S. DOWELL.

On previous pages I have mentioned this character as "Uncle Ben" Dowell, the postmaster. He was a Kentuckian, who served through the war with Mexico, and at its close settled at El Paso in the "forties" and married at Ysleta.

He was an illiterate man, but of great force of character. One day in the early "fifties" he did good work by killing, in a street fight, a desperado who was known to have broken into the Customs House and robbed the safe and who, with a party of men like himself, was defying the authorities. Dowell and I became friends, but when the question of secession arose he went wild on that subject and was, in part, responsible for my arrest as an "abolitionist," and we were bitter enemies for several years.

He left El Paso with the retreating Texans just before we (the Union troops) took possession of that place in 1862. He returned to Juarez, and we met there several times but did not speak to each other. Finally Dowell wrote me a letter (printed below) which led to a renewal of our friendship, which continued till his death:

"Paso Del Norte (Juarez), Mexico, October 12th, 1864.

"Mr. W. W. Mills: Dear Sir—You may think strange to receive a communication from me, but as circumstances alter cases I will proceed with my subject. I left Sherman, Texas, on the 27th, day of December last with the intention of making my way, if possible, to El Paso, as I did not think my life safe in Texas out of the

Confederate ranks, which service did not suit me. I came here with the full intention of crossing over to El Paso to live, if I could get admission by complying with all that might be required of a citizen. But when I arrived here I commenced to talk with some old friends, and changed my notion for a time. I am now tired of living a dog's life, and I wish to live on your side of the river.

"I hope you will pass over in forgetfulness any hard feelings you might have entertained toward me, and report favorably to the commanding officer at your post. Please let me hear from you by the bearer, and let this communication be confidential, and oblige, yours, etc.,

"B. S. DOWELL."

This letter was brought to my office by Uncle Ben's little daughter Mary, and I immediately replied that I would be his friend, and without consulting the commanding officer, Col. George W. Bowie, I invited Dowell to come to my house. He came the next day, bringing his very valuable race mare, the apple of his eye, and he told me that his brother "Nim," whom I also knew, was a Union man and had attempted to escape from Texas and had been followed and killed by the Confederates.

While we were talking over old times and thinking no harm a file of the guard appeared at my door and informed me that they had orders to take Dowell to the guard house and his mare to the Government corral.

I was, of course, indignant. What? Federal bayonets shoved into *my* door after all that I had gone through? In this frame of mind I called on Colonel Bowie and gave him what in these days might be called "a song and dance." I told the Colonel that Dowell was ready to take the oath prescribed in President Lincoln's amnesty proclamation, but he replied that he would not permit his adjutant to administer the oath, but out of consideration for me he would permit my friend to return to Mexico with his mare. He went, but the following day I wrote out the proper paper for Dowell and he swore to it before Henry J. Cunniffe, United States Consul at Juarez, and I took my friend and introduced him to Colonel Bowie as a fully fledged American citizen!

The Colonel gracefully acknowledged that he was beaten, and Dowell remained with us. Dowell owned some desirable town lots in El Paso, which were saved from confiscation by his timely oath of allegiance. These lots were of little value at the time, but he managed to hold them till the advent of the railroads and the first El Paso boom, so that he lived poor and died wealthy.

The Dowell race mare proved useful; and here I state some facts of which I am neither proud nor ashamed. Uncle Ben assured me that she could outrun any quarter nag that would come to El Paso, and we formed a partnership under which he furnished the animal and the "horse sense" and I the money for the stakes. The race track was nearly along the line of West Overland street, the outcome being at its junction with El Paso street. Race animals were brought from California, New Mexico and Colorado to contest with us, and in four years we won several thousand dollars *without losing a race.*

I withdrew from the partnership and quit all such business after my marriage in 1869.

BRAD. DAILY.

While the hostile Texans were approaching Fort Craig I was a lieutenant and aide-de-camp to the commanding officer at that post, Gen. B. S. Roberts. The General directed me to try to find some intelligent, faithful citizen acquainted with the country to go as a spy to El Paso (from whence I had escaped) and bring him reliable information of the Texan forces in that vicinity. Brad. Daily, whom I had known well at El Paso, was at the time wagonmaster in charge of Ochoa's train, and in camp near the post. He was an old frontiersman, an Indian fighter, and had often been employed as a guide by United States army officers. I knew that he was a Southerner, but I knew that when a man of that class took the Union side he could be trusted, and I knew that he possessed every other qualification for the dangerous service. I visited his camp and asked him casually what he thought about the war. He replied that while he was a Southern man "Uncle Sam" had always treated him right and that he would stand by the Government. I then told him what was wanted, and he agreed to undertake the enterprise.

I took him to the General and vouched for him, and he was supplied with two good horses and plenty of gold, and at midnight he started on his mission. I, of course, gave him no letters but referred him to two of my friends, whom he also knew very well, Don José Ma. Uranga, then Prefect of Juarez, and my former employer, Mr. Vincente St. Vrain, a merchant of El Paso. Daily entered Juarez in the night and went to the Prefect's house, where he remained concealed for a week or more, only going out at night. He met St. Vrain and other Union men at the Prefect's house, and he actually prowled through Fort Bliss of nights disguised as a Mexican peon, and came away as well informed about the number of troops and other matters at that post as the Texas officers themselves. He brought an unsigned letter which I knew to be in St. Vrain's handwriting, giving wholesale military information. This letter, had its contents been known to the Confederates, would have cost my friend St. Vrain his life. Said letter has been published by the United States Government in the "Records of the Rebellion."

On his return Daily rode in the dark into a camp of Indians and came into Fort Craig with an arrowhead in his shoulder. He was paid $2,500 for his two weeks' work, which he deposited with the Quartermaster, and was employed as a guide during the campaign which ensued.

This man Daily was at times addicted to drink, and when intoxicated would gamble. One night an officer awakened me and informed me that Daily was at the sutler's store drunk and gambling and being robbed. I went to the store and found him in company with some gamblers (camp followers) vainly trying, with their help, to sign his name to an order on the Quartermaster for two thousand dollars. I tore the paper into bits and took Daily away. The next morning I reported the facts to General Roberts, and he directed me to take a file of the guard and destroy all the intoxicating liquor at the store, place all loafers I found about the store in the guard house, and lock the store and bring the key to him. The order was executed. About a dozen "loafers" were provided with quarters in the guard house;

barrels of whisky were rolled out and the heads driven in and hundreds of bottles were smashed. Some of the soldiers scooped up whisky in their hands and drank it.

After the campaign Daily with his savings became a respectable and successful merchant of Las Cruces, N. M., and twenty years later was sued for that two thousand dollar debt. I was interrogated as a witness, and testified to the facts as I have written them above. Daily won the suit.

JOHN LEMON.

In 1861 John Lemon, a gentleman of about my own age, resided with his wife and children at La Mesilla, N. M., fifty miles north of El Paso. I was not then acquainted with Mr. Lemon, but soon after my escape to Fort Craig from the Confederates at Fort Bliss in 1861, and after the Confederates had taken possession of La Mesilla, Lemon and one Jacob Applezoller and a Kentuckian named Critendon Marshall, were arrested and placed in the guard house as "Union men." One midnight these three were taken from the guard house by the guard and a party of citizens to a bosque and Marshall was hung by the neck until he was dead. Applezoller was also suspended by a rope, but for some reason was cut down before death ensued, and I believe is still living in New Mexico. Lemon and Applezoller were taken back to the guard house and some time later Lemon made his escape and joined the Union people at Fort Craig, as I had done a few weeks earlier. There we two refugees met for the first time, and there commenced an intimate friendship which continued to the time of his death by assassination, which occurred at La Mesilla about ten years later. After the Confederates were driven from the frontier Mr. Lemon returned to his home, where he acquired wealth and popularity, being repeatedly elected County Judge. One night in 1865 an express came to my house at El Paso with a note from Lemon requesting me to come immediately to La Mesilla, but without intimating why. I went at once, and Lemon explained that he had been slandered by Col. Samuel J. Jones (a neighbor) and that he was determined to make Jones retract or kill him. I called on Jones as Lemon's friend, and he referred me to a young frontier lawyer then almost unknown but who has since become very wealthy and very prominent in the politics of the nation, attaining the very highest offices excepting only those of President and Vice President.

This gentleman acted as Jones' friend, and it was due to his fairness and firmness that Jones signed a retraction and a fight was avoided. I am proud to say that this friend of Jones' became my friend, and remains so to this day. This was Stephen B. Elkins. Of all the men of the frontier with whom I have been associated I liked John Lemon best, and I think him the most admirable character of them all. He possessed all the best qualities of the frontiersman with none of their vices. He was *with* us, but not *of* us. He was strictly temperate, perfect in habits and morals, and yet a genial, sympathetic companion and faithful friend, and behind a manner almost as modest and quiet as a Quaker's there rested a personal courage and resolution equal to that of Andrew Jackson. In 1870 Mr. Lemon's party (the Republicans) had gained a county election, and while he was going to join the procession which was celebrating he was struck in the head with a bludgeon from behind and died a few days later.

"BOB" CRANDALL AS A DAMPHOOL.

While I was collector of customs at El Paso a good friend of mine, Captain Crandall, had been honorably discharged from the Union army and had located at Tucson.

Crandall came to El Paso and stopped at my house and informed me that his father had died in Indiana and that he ("Bob") was en route there to get his portion of the estate, and he hoped to return pretty well fixed. After several months Bob returned, and came to my house looking dejected and rather seedy. He told me that others had administered on his father's estate before he arrived and had got away with it all and that he was destitute.

I asked my friend what he proposed to do? He said he would work his way back to Tucson and commence life anew. The next morning I asked him to accompany me to my office, and as we walked I said: "Bob, as soon as we get to the office I will write your appointment as deputy collector of customs at Tucson at a salary of $1,800 a year, and I will advance you a month's salary." My friend paused and when he spoke there were tears in his *voice.* "Mills," he said, "do you know that I am a Democrat?" "Yes," I replied, "but is that any reason why you should be a damphool?" "Well," replied the Captain, speaking slowly, "I don't know that it is, but sometimes it appears to me *that it amounts to about the same thing.*" He got the appointment and years later died at Tucson. I told this story to a mixed audience in a political speech at the Court House in El Paso, and feel sure that it did not offend even the most enthusiastic Democrat.

ROBBERY OF MY HOUSE IN 1865—INDIAN TRAILERS.

In 1865 I lived, a bachelor, in a house which is still standing on the lot at the corner of San Francisco and Chihuahua streets. My sleeping room was in the southeast corner of the house with a window opening on the back yard (corral) to the south. My brother, E. A. Mills, and a negro servant slept in the back rooms of the house.

One day a number of Mexicans were carrying and stacking adobes in that back yard and of course had left five thousand foot tracks. That night I locked the front door of my room as usual and went to visit some friends. On my return to my room about midnight I unlocked the door and struck a light, to find that everything movable which I had left in the room had been removed. Every article of clothing, bric-a-brac, a Mexican blanket worth $100, and all such articles as a gentleman keeps in his private room were gone. If any reader has had a similar experience he knows what a foolish, puzzled feeling comes over him on making the discovery.; he first thinks he has gotten into the wrong room, then that somebody has played a practical joke on him, and must be at that moment watching and laughing at him. Suddenly the unpleasant truth flashes upon him that he has been robbed. Such was my experience.

Well, I awakened my brother, started him over the river for some Indian trailers, and then went to sleep. Two Indians came and lay down before my door till daybreak, and then called me and made an examination. They informed me that one lone thief had entered my room at the window and packed my property into a big round bundle, which he had lifted and dragged through the window. It was, of course, impossible to follow the thief's tracks through the corral where so many men had been tramping the previous day, but the Indians had seen a few of his footprints near the window, and *that was enough.*

They started to walk slowly in a circle around my premises, going in opposite directions with their eyes fixed on the ground. Presently one of them whistled. He had found the trail. The Indians, and I with them, followed this trail for an hour, through many meanderings, and finally arrived at an old adobe house near where the Pierson Hotel now stands. The ground was dry and none but an expert trailer could see a single track. The Indians walked around the house in a circle, at some distance from it, and informed me that the thief was inside, and refused to act further because they feared they might be assassinated by some of his pals. I entered the house and found two Mexican women, who told me that no man was there or had been there. I searched all the rooms and found no one, and so reported to the Indians. They said: "He went in. He did not come out. *He is inside.*" Making a more thorough search, I found the gentleman concealed in one of the rooms under a stack of beef hides.

He was a noted thief of Juarez. None of the stolen articles were found on him or in the house. Our prisons were insecure and the courts were not much safer, and I turned the man over to the "boys," who somehow convinced him that this was not a good locality for him, and he was heard of no more.

Several weeks later a little Mexican boy came to me

greatly excited and told me that he had seen a corner of my Mexican blanket projecting from a little sandhill near the house where the thief had been caught. Every article which had been stolen was found tied in that blanket and uninjured. The Indians in going around the house to find any trail which might be going out had taken too wide a circle, or they would have found where the articles were buried.

ATTEMPT AT ASSASSINATION IN 1867—A MYSTERY.

In 1867 I lived in my home on San Antonio street, two blocks west of where the Court House now stands. There were two rooms opening on the street, one of which had a spare bed in it for guests and was never used by me. Back of this room, with a partition door between and with a door and window giving into the back yard, was my own private room—the room in which I habitually slept. My brother slept in another part of the house. Of course it was my habit to lock the door opening into the back yard, around which yard there was an adobe wall about six feet high.

I had some bitter enemies among the Americans at that time, some avowed and others secret, as I afterward learned.

On the night in question I retired as usual in my own room, and, strangely enough, on *this* night of all nights, must have neglected to lock the door. I awoke during the night and for some reason which I have never been able to explain to myself, a fancy seized me to sleep in the guest's room. I went there, taking my pistol and candle, leaving my watch on the table and all my other belongings handy for any one who might come to take them, provided *theft* were the object. I supposed the back door to be locked, and closed the partition door between the guest's room and the bedroom I had left. I awoke again with a consciousness that some one was in the room. I had not heard any sound. I could not possibly see anything, yet I was *sure* that I was not alone. I was wide awake, was not alarmed; my feeling was rather one of wonder.

I said aloud: "Wait a moment; I will strike a light." I did so, and saw a man, in his shirt sleeves, going through the partition door into the bedroom, and closing it after him. I did not see his face. I seized my pistol and followed through my bedroom and heard some one scramble over the wall and into the street. Rain had fallen that night, and any man, in climbing into the back yard, must have soiled his hands with mud and dirt from the wall.

I called my brother and we found that no article of my belongings had been disturbed, but my pillow and bed clothes were smeared and blackened, and we distinctly saw the prints of a man's fingers! The object was clearly not theft. It is not usual to awaken a man to steal his property. *That man's hand surely held a knife and he was feeling for my heart!* I have always felt sure that the man who entered my room was not an enemy, but a hireling. But who was the instigator, and what the motive? That remains a mystery to this day. But to me a greater mystery still is *why* did I change my room that night? *How* did I know that there was some one in the room where I was sleeping, when I could neither see him nor hear him? "Quein sabe"!

FATE OF MY CUSTOM-HOUSE DEPUTIES.

Of the thirty or more young men who were from time to time employes of mine in this Customs District while I was collector (1863 to 1869), I believe only two are now living (1900), my brother, E. A. Mills of Mexico, and Maximo Aranda of San Elizario. Seven of them met violent deaths, four while in the service. Here is the record: Mills (no relative of mine), killed by Indians near Tucson in 1864; Virgil Marstin, killed by Indians near Silver City in 1865; John F. Stone, killed by Indians near Fort Bowie in 1869; James Taylor, killed by robbers near where the El Paso smelter is now located, in 1866; Judge John Lemon, killed by a mob at Mesilla, N. M., in 1869; Moses Kelly, shot to death at Presidio del Norte, about 1870; Abraham Lyon, shot to death at Tucson; A. J. Fountain was recently murdered on the plains near Las Cruces, N. M., and A. H. French died insane in asylum at Austin.

CHANGE OF CUSTOMS DISTRICT—SAMUEL J. JONES. (1863.)

My last military service was as quartermaster and commissary at District headquarters at Santa Fe, in 1862. In the summer of that year, General Canby granted me a leave of absence for sixty days, and I visited Washington City and received from President Lincoln my commission as collector of customs along with his personal thanks and good wishes.

The collection district of Paso del Norte then comprised only the Territories of New Mexico and Arizona, the collector's office being at Las Cruces, N. M. El Paso county belonged to the Galveston District, with a deputy at El Paso—A. B. O'Bannon, a Confederate. But Congress, at my suggestion, passed an act, approved March 3, 1863, attaching El Paso county to that district, "Provided that the collector should reside at El Paso." Thus, by my efforts, El Paso became the permanent residence of collectors of customs, and as a result, later on, obtained its fine Government building! Col. Samuel J. Jones was then collector of customs at Las Cruces. This Jones was prominent and in some respects a remarkable character. He was the notorious "Sheriff Jones" during the border troubles in Kansas in 1856, when the attempt was made to make Kansas a slave State, and was then called a "border ruffian." Jones was a man of education, of fine personal appearance, and with a reputation for courage which had never been questioned. It fell to my lot to be the first to call him down, and I did it successfully and still have the hostile letters which passed between us, but I refrain from recording the particulars of that incident in my life. Jones had been appointed collector of customs by President Buchanan, but had taken the side of secession.

On my return from Washington, Jones refused to deliver to me the books and property of the office, and correspondence, quarrels and threats followed, and we became bitter enemies. But he yielded what I demanded. Twenty years later I met Colonel Jones at Silver City, old, poor and paralyzed, just able to walk about, but only able to articulate the words "yes, yes," and "no, no." Knowing his condition, I gave him my hand, which he grasped eagerly, and that night he signified to me that he desired me to occupy the same room with him, which I did.

CAPTAINS SKILLMAN AND FRENCH.

Capt. Henry Skillman resided near El Paso for many years previous to the Civil War. He was a Kentuckian, a man of magnificent physique, over six feet tall, wearing long, sandy hair and a beard flowing to his girdle.

He was an Indian fighter, mail contractor, and a guide and scout for the United States troops and for wagon trains through the Indian country. He was the Kit Carson of this section. He was highly esteemed, almost beloved, by the people of the valley, of both races.

He had one fault. At rare intervals he would get very drunk and become wild and ride his horse into the stores and saloons of the village, firing his pistol the while, and order everybody to close up, as he desired to run the town himself. Then he would go home and sober up and come to town, pay the damages and apologize to every one and then go about his business.

As an offset to this peculiarity he would not allow any other man to play the same role, when he was around. Once, when a stranger attempted it, and everybody, including the peace officers, was terrified, Skillman was notified, and came up, sober, took away the ruffian's arms, boxed his jaws, and notified him to leave town, which he did.

On another occasion, 1857, when my brother Anson had accused two El Paso men of counterfeiting, they plotted to assassinate him on the street, and then to swear that the killing was accidental. As they approached my brother, pretending to be very drunk, Skillman saw and understood the maneuver, and, springing to the rescue, called out: "Look out there, Mills; they are going to kill you."

When the secession talk commenced, it was known to me and to a few others that Skillman, although his associates were nearly all Confederates, inclined strongly to the Union side; but he finally "went with his State," and in 1864 he, with a small band of Confederates, was acting as a scout and keeping up communication between San Antonio and the Confederate colony at Juarez, Mexico, near El Paso.

General Carleton, then in command of New Mexico, decided upon the capture of Skillman and his party, and for that service he selected Capt. Albert H. French, of the California Volunteer Cavalry.

General Carleton was present at El Paso when French left on this dangerous expedition, and I KNOW that he gave French special instructions to bring Skillman in alive "if possible," and I know the reason for this order.

French was a Boston man. He was as large and as well formed as Skillman, and, like him, was of sandy complexion, hair and beard.

Skillman and his party were near Presidio del Norte en route for Juarez when Captain French (himself unseen) discovered them and watched them go into camp (April 3, 1864).

At midnight, French, with a portion of his little command, including two citizens of San Elizario, *crawled* into Skillman's camp, and, rising to their feet, called for surrender. Skillman arose, armed, and refused, when French shot him dead.

In the volley which followed two more of Skillman's party were killed and two wounded. The others surrendered and were brought to San Elizario.

There were citizens of El Paso county in each of these parties, some of whom are still living.

I regret to see that Col. George W. Baylor has been led, by false information, no doubt, into doing some injustice to the memory of the gallant Captain French.

In a late communication to the El Paso Herald the colonel says: "Captain French killed or rather massacred Capt. James Skillman, who was in the C. S. A. and on picket duty in the Davis mountains. They had been personal friends, and through treachery French had located Skillman and killed him. It has been said that the matter so preyed on French's mind that it became unbalanced before his death."

Colonel Baylor is himself an old soldier, justly proud of his record, and he should be careful not to place too much reliance on the statements of others. It is impossible that French and Skillman could have been "friends," as the colonel states, because they had never met each other till that fateful night. And again, the colonel shows lack of information by speaking of Skillman as "James" instead of Henry.

Captain French's conduct was soldierly and commendable.

FURNISHING ARMS TO MEXICO—1865.

Early in 1865, when the Mexican patriots, under President Juarez, were hard pressed by the French troops and the forces of the usurping Emperor Maximilian, my friend, Don Juan Zubiran, then collector of customs at Juarez, brought a gentleman to my office and introduced him as a confidential agent of the Mexican government.

This gentleman did not hesitate to confide to me that his mission was to purchase arms and ammunition for use against the invaders of his country. This was a delicate matter because, if United States officials favored his scheme, it might have involved our government in difficulty, or even war with France, with which country we were friendly, although all loyal Americans, from the President down, sympathized deeply with Mexico in her struggle for existence. I could not betray this gentleman's secret, and he proceeded to Santa Fe, New Mexico, where Gen. James H. Carleton was in command of the United States troops, and thence to Washington City; and it was not long before several hundred stands of arms in New Mexico were condemned as being "unserviceable" and were moved down to Las Crues, fifty miles north of El Paso, and advertised for sale at public auction. These rifles, with ammunition, were purchased by my friend, Don Juan Zubiran, and were to be delivered to the Governor of Sonora at Conalitos, in the State of Chihuahua, near the Sonora line, and were to be received and paid for there. *Somehow* these arms found their way over the boundary line to

Conalitos, and now comes the interesting part of their story—if it has any interest at all.

Mr. Zubiran was about to send an express to Hermisillo, the capital of Sonora, to notify Governor —— that the arms were ready for delivery, but it would have been a long and dangerous journey, and as I had a deputy collector of customs (one McWard) at Tucson, nearer Hermisillo, Mr. Zubiran requested me to forward his letter under cover to McWard, and ask him to send it by messenger to Governor —— and ask him to reply through the same channels. This was done, and in due time there came a reply to Mr. Zubiran, written on the printed letter-head paper of the "Executive of the State of Sonora," signed by the Governor, and to every appearance genuine. But the contents of this letter were startling. It stated that the Governor regretted that he could not receive or pay for the arms; that the Mexican cause was hopeless, and it advised my friend Zubiran (than whom Mexico had no stancher patriot) to give in his allegiance to the Empire of Maximilian!

We were astounded; but there was the fact in plain black and white.

Some weeks later an express rider came in great haste from the Governor of Sonora, with a letter to Mr. Zubiran, asking why such delay about the rifles, and urging haste, and stating that the money to pay for them was already at Conalitos.

We finally got at the explanation of this chapter of misunderstandings. A former Governor of Sonora had espoused the cause of Maximilian, had fled from his country, and taken refuge at Tucson, carrying with him some of the stationery of the State, and had become intimate with Deputy McWard, who had betrayed to him the contents of Zubiran's letter, thus enabling him to prepare and forward the bogus reply, with such appearance of genuineness.

The arms were delivered and paid for, and it is needless to state that the faithless Deputy McWard lost his official head.

PRESIDENT JUAREZ' GOVERNMENT AT CIUDAD JUAREZ, NEAR EL PASO—1865-66.

For more than a year, in 1865 and 1866, the village of Paso del Norte (now Ciudad Juarez), opposite El Paso, was the actual capital of the Mexican Republic. Benito Juarez, the patriot President, with his Cabinet and a little remnant of his army, had been driven from his capital by the French troops and the Mexican adherents of Maximilian, and were making a last stand on this frontier, the French troops having possession of the city of Chihuahua, only two hundred and twenty-five miles to the southward.

The writer happened at that time to occupy the most important United States office on the frontier. He spoke Juarez's own language well, and Juarez knew that he sympathized as deeply with the republican cause in Mexico as the Mexican President sympathized with the cause of the Republic of the United States. Our Government had at that time no minister near the Juarez Government. I visited the President very often. Was it strange if we held many conversations, in which each confided to the other his hopes and fears, as to the success or failure of the two simultaneous efforts then being made to destroy the two greatest Republics in the world—our own countries? In January, 1866, I informed President Juarez that I contemplated a journey to Washington City, and before I started he confided to me a letter to the Mexican Minister, Señor Romero, and also one to his wife, who, with her two daughters, were then at Romero's house in Washington, refugees from their own country.

A VISIT TO WASHINGTON—POLITICAL CONTESTS.

This journey was made by stage coach via Santa Fe as far as Kansas City, thirteen hundred miles, in mid-winter, and was not without interesting incidents, one of which I will relate. We left Santa Fe with six passengers, Judge S. Watts, two young ladies, two merchants and myself. There was also the stage driver and the driver of a wagon which carried our provisions and baggage. The weather, for the greater portion of the time, was intensely cold, the ground being covered with snow. We slept under a roof only twice during the journey of twelve days.

My brother, Anson Mills, was then a cavalry captain in the army, but I had not heard from him for many months, and had not the slightest idea in what part of the country he might be. One very cold day, about noon, when approaching the Arkansas River, we met a train of wagons bound for Santa Fe, and the wagon-master informed us that he had the day before been attacked by a party of Indians at the crossing of the Arkansas, but had stood them off, and had moved on, uninjured. He advised us to return to Santa Fe, but, incredible as it may seem, we decided to proceed on our journey. I do not call this courage; to me, after so many years, it appears more like foolhardiness!

Nearing the river, but before we could see down into the valley, we saw, far to our right, and apparently flanking us, two men with rifles, whom we supposed might be Indians.

The coach was halted, we four male passengers, with our arms, moved toward the strangers and beckoned them to approach. They did so, and I soon recognized the familiar uniform of United States soldiers! I asked, "Where are you camped?" Reply: "Down yonder at the crossing." "Who is in command?" "Captain Mills." "What Mills?" *"Captain Anson Mills."*

The ladies slept that night in the captain's tent and we brothers, by the camp fire, told each other our adventures since we had separated at El Paso, five years before, each to take his chances in the desperate game of war.

Captain Mills gave me his application for promotion to present at Washington, and after the stage had started he called to me: "Get me a leave of absence, and I will go to Washington and return your visit."

Arrived in Washington, I presented the application for promotion to Gen. John B. Steedman, who indorsed it thus: "Captain Mills served on my staff for three years. He is the best officer of his rank I ever knew; intelligent, efficient and fearless. I recommend him for promotion."

A few days later I went with some New Mexican friends to call on General Grant, who was then Secretary of war. I told the General about meeting my brother, and asked a leave of absence for him. The General replied that such applications must come through the regular channels. I showed the Secretary the application for promotion, with Steedman's indorsement, and told him something of our troubles at El Paso at the outbreak of the Rebellion. He read the papers and seemed pleased, but continued talking with my friends and dispatching business. On rising to take our leave, I told General Grant that I was sorry not to meet my brother at Washington, but I could not complain, as I saw good reasons for the refusal. To which he replied: "The telegram has gone, sir; your brother will be here in a few days."

He came, and got his promotion also.

Soon after this I was summoned to the State Department for an interview with the Secretary, William H. Seward. He asked many questions about President Juarez and his cause, and about the real sentiment of the Mexican people, and about their probable ability to drive Maximilian and the French out of Mexico "without assistance."

Mr. Seward asked me about our consul at Juarez, Henry J. Cuniffe. I replied that he was an able and patriotic gentleman.

The Secretary then said that in the absence of the United States Minister, our consul ought to have an extra allowance of money for expenses during the Mexican President's stay at Juarez, and asked me what amount I thought would be sufficient.

I replied $2,500 a quarter, and the Secretary said that would not be too much, and if the consul would make requisitions they would be honored.

I wrote my friend Cuniffe immediately.

This was before the days of "Retrenchment and Reform."

Now came one of my hardest battles. My term of four years as collector of customs at El Paso, under Lincoln, was about to expire, and there was objection to my reappointment—*there always is*—but in this case there was a serious charge of misconduct in office to the effect that I had permitted the exportation of large quantities of arms and ammunition from my district into Mexico to be used against the French, in violation of the instructions from my own Government and the neutrality laws; and "on the face of the returns" the charge appeared to be true, and my enemies believed my defeat *certain*.

Andrew Johnson was President. When I called on him, with some friends, to make my formal application, we met, by an awkward accident, a delegation of my enemies, and we "had it out" then and there. I stated my own case, and though the President was noncommittal, I felt sure of reappointment, though my friends did not. A few days afterward, when Judge Watts was talking to the President on other subjects, the President said: "Judge, where is your young friend from Texas? Is this his appointment which I signed to-day?" When told that it was, he said: "I intended from the first to appoint him. I like that young man."

In the Senate there was opposition to my confirmation. Senator Conness of California made a sensational speech against me in executive session, and presented what he called "proof." I saw the Senator personally and made some explanations, which it is not necessary, or proper, to repeat here, and he withdrew his opposition and moved my confirmation, and I was unanimously confirmed.

In May, 1866, the President's private secretary, Col. Henry Cooper, asked the Texas Republicans then in Washington to agree upon some Texan to be appointed "Visitor to West Point."

These appointments are strictly Presidential, not requiring confirmation by the Senate, and are much desired and sought after, being considered a high honor and a special favor from the chief executive of the nation. We met and selected a very distinguished Texan, Judge George W. Paschal, and sent up his name

A few days later Colonel Cooper said to one of our friends: "The President does not like the selection of Paschal. He says he is going to appoint Mills. Tell Mills to come and see him." I called and thanked the President, and had some conversation with him, but later gave my brother, Capt. Anson Mills, a letter to the President, requesting him to substitute his name for mine, which was done.

I have known and conversed with four Presidents—Lincoln, Johnson, Grant and McKinley—and have held office under all of them; but I knew Andy Johnson best, and I liked the rugged, stubborn Southerner, who had stood firm as a rock against rebellion in his own section. If I had been older, or bolder, I am vain enough to believe I might possibly have been of service to him. He had inherited his Cabinet from Mr. Lincoln, and some of them were, from the start, not very devoted to him personally. He was being flattered and cajoled by his late enemies, and he had been fretted and angered by certain Republican leaders, "wise men of the East," who believed that no good could come out of Nazareth, and he was about to make the mistake of his life—*the break with his party*. I was pleased when, years later, he came to the United States Senate, supported by the votes of his best and truest friends—the Union people of Tennessee.

RECONSTRUCTION—CONSTITUTIONAL CONVENTION OF 1868-69.

In 1868 I was elected to represent El Paso county in the State Constitutional Convention, which was to meet at Austin in May of that year, to frame a constitution under which Texas might be readmitted into the Union. At the start I was opposed for that office by Major Joseph Smith, a popular Democrat, who had been honorably discharged from the United States military service at El Paso, but early in the contest I badgered him into saying that if he found a single "Nigger" in the convention, he would resign.

I then suggested to the Mexican audience that if he had that much race prejudice, he would not do to represent *them*. Major Smith soon saw certain defeat before him, and withdrew, and I was unanimously elected.

During April of that year, I went in a buggy, with a single companion, Hon. W. P. Bacon, Judge of our district, to San Antonio, en route to Austin, seven hundred and forty miles, in seventeen days, without change of animals (two horses). We "camped out" and did our own cooking, and traveled much at night, because marauding Indians were then abundant on that route. I arrived at Austin a total stranger to every soul in that capital. The convention had ninety delegates, only ten of whom were Democrats. There were nine colored delegates, a large contingent of carpetbaggers, and several new recruits to the Republican party, who claimed from the day of their conversion to be more "loyal" to that party than any of us. But about one-half of the body were able, representative, old-time Texans, who had taken the Union side of the secession question and had become Republicans. These were led by Gov. A. J. ("Jack") Hamilton, a man of Southern birth, once a slave-owner, who had been from the start the most prominent, boldest and most eloquent of the Union men of Texas, if not of the whole South. He was a member of Congress in 1861, and denounced secession both there and at home, and later was appointed a brigadier general and Provisional Governor of Texas by President Lincoln, and had gained a national reputation as an orator. And now the usual thing happened. "He who surpasses or subdues mankind must look down on the hate of those below." The small men in the convention combined to down the greatest one.

A resolution was passed the first day of the convention, without opposition, requiring all delegates to take what was then known as the "Ironclad Oath." This would have excluded several delegates who had, in one way or another, given aid and comfort to the rebellion.

The next day, Mills of El Paso, a Republican, moved to reconsider that resolution and to admit all who had been elected by the people. He urged that we were not officers of the United States, but of Texas, and scarcely that, because we could do nothing which would bind any one. Our work would have to be approved by the people, and then by Congress, etc., etc.

Governor Hamilton came to the rescue and Mills' motion was passed and all elected delegates were admitted. (The published records of the convention bear out the above statement.) And now the first charge was heard against Governor Hamilton, both in Texas and at Washington, that he had "sold out to the rebels."

The opponents of Governor Hamilton had the tact to

put forward, as their leader, Col. E. J. Davis, a Texas Union man, who had done good service during the war, and against whom nothing can be said except that he was inordinately ambitious, vain, vindictive, and that he was then, and for years after, surrounded and influenced by as lordly a set of unscrupulous adventurers as ever tyrannized over or wronged the people of any Southern State. He and Morgan Hamilton, a brother of Jack Hamilton, were almost the only leaders of respectability in the whole "Davis party."

The three questions upon which the Davis Republicans and the Hamilton Republicans wrangled so long in that convention were these:

1st. Davis contended that all who had participated in the Rebellion should be disfranchised. Hamilton opposed.

2d. Davis contended that all laws passed by the Legislature during the Rebellion were null and void, *ab initio.*

Hamilton contended that only such laws as contravened the Constitution and laws of the United States were void.

3d. Davis contended for a division of Texas into three States, and Hamilton opposed.

(The proposition to divide Texas was finally killed on motion of the writer of these chapters, and if any Texan thinks that the State was not then in danger of being divided, let him remember old Virginia.)

Hamilton won on all three of these propositions, and a constitution was framed in accordance with his views, and submitted to the people. I quote below a report of the last day's stormy session of this memorable convention, by Whilden, the brilliant correspondent of the Galveston News:

"TEXAS CONVENTION.

"Austin, Texas, February 8, 1869.

"Special to the Galveston News.

"Precisely at what point to begin I am in doubt. This convention, which we thought was to give civil government to Texas and to which we necessarily attached some dignity, has in the end proved itself to be a farce on the civilization of the nineteenth century. Jack Hamilton and a few others did all that genius could do to turn its purposes to legitimate ends. Partially they failed; but in that failure they left the impress of brains upon the wild waste of passion which this convention has given to the world. * * * All mortal things shall ever have an ending, and this convention is as all other mortal things.

"Strategic movements on the part of Davis and Hamilton have filled up the time. Between these two men there can be no comparison. * * *

"On last Friday night the cloud burst, and for a few moments the curse of heaven seemed to hang as a pillar of flame over the convention hall.

"Stern as Davis is, he quivered when Mills of El Paso tore from his bosom the thin gauze with which he hoped to hide the dark, selfish and damning purposes of his heart. Yes, he quivered, but it was for a while only. The devil never deserts his own for a long time at once. Davis rallied and poured the long pent-up passion of his heart upon Mills. Confusion ensued. The issue was now made. Davis was right and Mills very wrong, or Davis was wrong and Mills the Nemesis of the night. A majority of the convention agreed with Mills. But Davis has his tools. The convention had one more than a quorum. This quorum must be broken or Davis meets a Waterloo defeat. Two of Davis tools resigned their seats then and there. Thus was a quorum, under the standing rules, broken, and fortune for a while declared for Davis.

"But Hamilton was not thus to be defeated. He brought all his forces up against the political traitors, raised a point of order as to whether a quorum consisted of a majority of ninety members, which the convention ought to have had, had every delegate been in his seat, or of a majority of those who, at that time, were entitled to seats. Plausibility and common sense were on Hamilton's side. Davis' wrath was terrible. Mills must be punished. The convention could not see it through his spectacles, and he ordered the sergeant-at-arms to take Mills in custody. It was a wordy order. Davis, seeing his inevitable defeat, on his own motion, declared that the convention, as no quorum was present, stood adjourned till next day at 10 o'clock, and, with the mien of a lieutenant of his satanic majesty, left the rostrum.

"Before he had gotten half way down the aisle, Armstrong of Lamar had been elected president. Davis ordered the doorkeeper to open the doors so that members could go out. The doorkeeper refused.

"Then ensued a scene which cannot be described. Hamilton arose and spoke under all the excitement of the evening—spoke as only those can speak who are orators born—spoke until, if I had been in Davis' place, I would have prayed that the capitol might crush upon me and hide my awful shame."

The constitution was then adopted as a whole and this revolutionary attempt to break up the convention and prevent the reconstruction of the State and her readmission into the Union met a humiliating defeat.

The good General Canby, being then in command of the Department, approved of our course of action and submitted the constitution to the people.

Three days later, February 8, 1869, at Austin, Texas, the writer married Mary, eldest daughter of Governor A. J. Hamilton, who in this year of Grace 1900, still abides with him; but that is "another story," which he reserves for a later chapter.

HAMILTON-DAVIS CONTEST OF 1869—ADOPTION OF CONSTITUTION.

The reader may think it strange that I give so much space to so common an occurrence as a State election, but the explanation is simple. It was the first reasonable attempt to carry our State back into the Union. The Democrats had made one effort and had failed, because they had offended the dominant sentiment of the country by "Apprentice Laws," and other measures which virtually reduced the freedman to a state of slavery, and by electing to the United States Senate a man who had presided over the convention which carried Texas out of the Union. Because of this failure, the Democrats, as a party, took no part in the second effort to reconstruct the State, but divided, those of them who voted at all, between the two Republican candidates.

Thousands of them sullenly refused to vote at all. It was therefore a contest between *men and ideas. The questions were all new.* True, there have been many State elections since then, but the results have all been foregone conclusions, so that the younger generation of Texans know nothing of the excitement, the strenuousness, the manliness, of a real contest for the political control of a great State.

Davis and his party publicly denounced this constitution as being "framed in the interest of rebels," and swore to defeat it either before the people or at Washington. Will the reader believe that a month later these same men publicly declared *in favor* of this same constitution, and for E. J. Davis as their candidate for Governor under it? But that is history.

Hamilton also became a candidate for Governor. Gen. J. J. Reynolds was in command of the Department of Texas, and the elections were held under military supervision. Although both candidates were Republicans, General Reynolds and others secured the support of the national administration and the Republican National Committee for the Davis faction.

This Reynolds, a stranger to the people of Texas, desired to make himself United States Senator from the State, and with that purpose in view, permitted the frauds which defeated Hamilton, and he (Reynolds) declared Davis elected by a majority of only seven hundred votes, several whole counties being denied by Reynolds the right to vote at all. The Davis Legislature *did,* later on, elect this same J. J. Reynolds to be Senator, but the Senate of the United States refused to admit him, and he was subsequently suspended from the army by sentence of a court-martial!

The State was admitted to the Union, Davis was inaugurated, and the notorious Twelfth Legislature convened. I had the honor to be elected a member of that memorable body, and also had the honor to be counted out by Reynolds.

MARRIAGE AND JOURNEY TO MY EL PASO HOME.

I do not know why it is that only in novels and posthumous writings do men speak much of their wives, and even the novel usually *ends* where I think it should *begin,* with the marriage. The man who writes of his own career usually treats the most important event of his life incidentally or in a casual way, and if he praises any woman it is usually his mother. I suppose there must be some good reason for this general rule, and I deviate from it only to say that for a third of a century my wife has been the best, the truest and the most constant friend I have known, and if these writings shall have any interest for even a few friendly readers, it will be largely due to the fact that she is still by my side, aiding me with her intelligent criticism and her finer fancy.

Well, on the 8th day of February, 1869, we were married, she, surrounded by her family and the friends of her youth, and a few disappointed beaux, and I, attended by Generals Canby and Carleton, with whom I had served in the army, and the Hon. William P. Bacon, then Judge of the El Paso District, who, though he encountered misfortune later on, was, I believe, an honest man and a true friend. Camped in a grove near the Hamilton residence was the "outfit" which had brought me from El Paso, consisting of an ambulance made by Dougherty of St. Louis, especially for such journeys over the plains, and much more comfortable and better adapted for ladies and families than even the fine, large Concord stage coaches. It would "make up" at night like a berth in a Pullman palace car. My pair of fine, large Kentucky mules, "Seymour" and "Blair," which were mine for ten years, hauled us over this long route four different times without fault or accident. "Johnnie," my faithful, watchful driver and companion, was on hand, and also a "Mozo" (Mexican servant) and a saddle horse. My other team of four horses awaited us at Fort Stockton, midway of the route, where the mules were to be left, to follow later to El Paso. The ambulance was a little arsenal. I had a repeating rifle, a shotgun and a pistol, and Johnnie a rifle and pistol.

The day after the wedding, I called on General Canby and asked for an escort of ten infantrymen and a Government wagon and team. The soldiers and our baggage and provisions were to ride in the wagon and the team was to be changed at each military post. The General at first suggested that I might take advantage of the escort of a certain army officer, Captain ——, whom we had both known in New Mexico, and whom I had once reported to the General as being unfaithful to his country. (I would not have objected to an out and out Confederate.) When I declined to travel with this gentleman, Canby replied: "Yes, I remember. You shall have an escort of your own."

And now we started westward over the long road of more than seven hundred miles to our El Paso home, where my wife was to see no familiar face except my own. But we had youth, and health, and hope, and self-reliance, and a faith in human nature, which, I regret to say, subsequent experience did not justify. But enough of that.

During the whole journey of twenty-three days we slept under a roof only three nights, and usually made our camp away from the mail stations (which could afford us no accommodations, anyhow), and in order to have better pasture for the animals.

Here let me say a word in behalf of the much-abused mule. You have been told that he will kick the hat off your head while you are on his back. This is a slander. A horse will kick when he is violently and cruelly treated, but a mule very seldom does, and ours were as gentle as pet dogs. They roamed unfettered and untethered about the camp day and night, but would come in at call.

On the Concho River we encountered herds of buffalo, now extinct in Texas, not so many as I had often seen on the Northern plains, but many—hundreds and thousands.

I never had the desire, as many had, to wantonly butcher these lubberly animals, but almost every man has inherited the hunter's instinct, and I indulged it to some extent, making the excuse that we needed fresh meat, as indeed we did.

Shooting antelope was far better sport, but these, like the buffalo and the wild deer and the Indian, will soon be but traditions, and there will be no frontier at all. Mrs. Mills had never seen an antelope, and the first one I shot fell some distance from the ambulance, and I called out, with some pride, "Send a couple of men to bring in this antelope." She repeated my command, mimicking my voice and manner, and then said, "Why don't you pick the thing up and bring it yourself?" She said she supposed it was about the size of a jack-rabbit.

A few days later I alone killed three of these animals within three hundred yards of our "train," and *in less than half a minute.* There were a hundred or more of them on the flat top of a little hill, and I climbed to the top unseen, and with a repeating rifle fired into the bunch at about thirty yards. They ran toward me, and I fired seven shots in quick succession with the result given above. The frightened, crazy herd of beautiful animals ran toward our little "train" and passed on each side of it and the colored soldier fired about twenty shots at them, but not one took effect. Although it was midwinter, the weather was pleasant with the exception of two or three cold days. There was no snow or rain on this whole trip.

At that time, thirty years ago, small bands of marauding Indians might be expected almost anywhere, and particularly as we approached the Rio Grande, and our chief care was to guard against surprise, which was almost our only danger. We saw none on this journey, but we passed several scenes of bloody tragedies, some of them quite recent. When we descended into the valley of the Rio Grande I pointed to a Mexican "jacál" and told Mrs. Mills that was the style of house we were to live in. She was silent for a long time, but when we drove up to my comfortable, well-furnished little home on San Antonio street, with the shade trees in front, and she set her feet upon the first plank floor ever laid down in El Paso, and saw the preparations which my good friend and neighbor, Mrs. Zabriskie, had made for her reception and comfort, she brightened up wonderfully.

Yes, other families also crossed these plains, but they were either army people for whom the Government furnished teams and provisions and attendants and protection, or others who traveled in the dusty rear of some freight train at a speed of about ten miles a day. Our voyages were mostly made independently, comfortably, and speedily, and without a single accident.

All depends upon thorough preparation, good judgment and constant vigilance.

Mrs. Mills' reception by the people of both races and on both sides of the river was very flattering, and I am sure it was sincere, and we spent nearly a year very happily at El Paso, but now (November, 1869) it was thought best that I should return to Austin to assist General Hamilton in his contest for the Governorship and control of the State. We returned with the same outfit with which we had come, except that we had no military escort, and Colonel Zabriskie went as our guest.

Soon after we left Fort Davis we saw far to our right a party of mounted Indians, how many we could not tell, but certainly too many for our small party. A company of infantry soldiers had left Fort Davis, going eastward, an hour before we did, and we had passed them on the road, so we knew they could not be far behind us, and we halted to await their arrival. The Indians also halted and gave us a free exhibition of fancy horsemanship and curious antics, until the gleaming rifles of the troops appeared on the road, when they scurried away around the mountain. We traveled in company with the soldiers until we reached Fort Stockton.

A year before I had sent five hundred gallons of wine of my own manufacture to each of the military posts, Davis and Stockton, and on arriving we found that it had all been sold at $5 per gallon, and Mrs. Mills stuffed the greenbacks into her little handsatchel for future use.

The postmaster at Fort Concho, "Jim" Trainer, whom I had never seen, had threatened to whip me on sight because he had been told that I had said he gave false receipts to the Mail Company, as other postmasters had done. After we got into camp near Concho I told my wife that I would go up to the sutler's store and see Mr. Trainer, and I remember her cheery words to me as I walked away: "Look out for yourself!"

Arrived at the store I entered and asked for Mr. Trainer. A good-looking, good-natured gentleman behind the counter replied that he was the man, and when I told him who I was he hesitated awhile and then invited me into the office, gave me a chair and a cigar, and after we had chatted awhile he asked me if I knew he had intended to thrash me. I told him yes, but that I had never spoken unkindly of him and did not know anything about his acts as postmaster. He said he had been the victim of liars, and presented me with a bottle of fine brandy and wished me a pleasant journey. Trainer was not a coward but had been played upon by my enemies.

ASSAULT BY KUHN AT FREDRICKSBURG.

When we arrived at Fredricksburg, sixty-five miles west of Austin, where Mr. Zabriskie left us for San Antonio, we stopped at Nimmit's Hotel for a day's rest, and Mrs. Mills and I were given a room upstairs. During the day I met in the hall of the hotel Albert Kuhn, who has been mentioned in my war story as the man who piloted the party of Texas soldiers who kidnapped me in Juarez in 1861, and who had received the reward for my capture. Kuhn had left El Paso with the Confederates in 1862, and I had not seen or heard of him for eight years. Kuhn was a very large man of rough and almost frightful appearance, and prided himself on being considered *bad*. He was a prototype of Mark Twain's "Mr. Arkansas." We passed each other without speaking, but when we met a second time in the back yard Kuhn said: "Mills, don't you know me?" I replied: "Yes." "Then why didn't you speak to me?" "Because I did not wish to do so." Kuhn then went to the bar and proceeded to get himself drunk. I told "Johnnie" what had occurred and instructed him to harness the team and be ready to proceed on our journey. I told my wife that Kuhn was at the hotel and that there might be trouble. I went down stairs again, armed, of course, and met Kuhn, but he made no demonstration. Mrs. Mills and I then went to the ambulance, Johnnie being already on the box, and Mrs. Mills got inside, but before I could take my seat Kuhn appeared with a cocked pistol in his hand and swore great oaths that if I did not get out he would kill me where I was.

What could I do? My wife was in as much danger as myself, so I attempted to descend from the carriage and make the best fight possible, but Mrs. Mills had more presence of mind than I, and catching hold of me she said to Kuhn: "You cowardly murderer, would you kill a man in the presence of his wife? Get away from here." Kuhn said he had great respect for ladies, but swore that he would kill me the first time we met. But we never met. If we had my opinion is that the chances would have been against him.

We drove only a few miles that evening and camped for the night about a quarter of a mile from the road and thinking that Kuhn might follow, I took position with my shotgun at a tree *near* the road and waited to give him both barrels of buckshot as soon as he should turn the corner of the fence. My old friend, Judge Cooley of Fredricksburg, says that Kuhn *did* saddle his horse that night and swore he would follow and kill me, but was restrained by others.

Now, what did this man want to quarrel with *me* about? I was the one who had been wronged. I give it up.

We arrived at Austin safe and well. The election resulted in the defeat of the Hamilton party as related elsewhere, and I made a campaign of several months in Washington City, where, though the wrong could not be fully righted, I was of some service to some of our defeated friends, and was somewhat successful in a business matter.

THIRD VOYAGE OVER THE PLAINS—ENEMIES AND PLOTS.

And now, April, 1871, we again turned our faces toward our El Paso home, in the hope of recuperating in other business what we had lost in politics, for my expenses had been very heavy.

I still held my town lots, and having faith in the future of El Paso I took out a license as a real estate agent ten years before any one else. "Seymour" and "Blair" and the amublance were still on hand, and I purchased another pair of very large mules (which we named "Insect" and "Fairy") and a wagon for our baggage, provision, etc., and employed two Mexican drivers. "Johnnie" was absent this time, but the *Mozo,* Lorenzo was still with us. The most important and interesting personage in our party was Hamilton Mills, aged twelve months, who had joined our family at Austin.

Governor Davis had given El Paso a new District Judge, S. B. Newcomb, and a new District Attorney, J. P. Hague, neither of whom had ever been heard of on the frontier. These and two adventurers asked permission to join our party, which was granted, and these four "tenderfeet" made the journey with us in a wagon drawn by two little mules. Our ideas as to traveling over the plains were so different that we sometimes separated for a day or night. They fondly believed that a "station" was a place where warm meals and clean beds and forage for animals were to be had, and their greatest anxiety was to "get in." We depended upon our mess chest for ourselves, and grassy camps for our animals, and fared much better.

Much depends upon selecting a good camp, and some of ours were very pleasant, and even beautiful, so that we had the appearance of a picnic party. I remember that sometimes we have made a long drive in order to reach some remembered nook where we had spent a night on former journeys, and we would drive into it with a feeling akin to coming home.

We reached the Pecos river at Horsehead crossing (where I had camped twelve years earlier with the Boundary Commission) at daybreak one morning. The river was swollen and the crossing dangerous. I first sent a man across on horseback, and then placing my wife and child in the ambulance I mounted the box and drove through the torrent, *leading the way for the four adult male tenderfeet.* Their cries to us when we had reached the western bank, "We can make it," "We can make it," were intended to cheer us, but really it was not a matter of the greatest importance to us whether they "made it" or not; and, could we have foreseen the future we might have felt still more indifferent. It is but fair to state that, later on Mr. Hayne forsook my enemies and became my friend and remained so till his death.

And now, arrived at my home, came the most trying days of my life. Up to this time the malignity of my enemies could affect only myself, but now my wife and child must suffer also. There were never more than a dozen of these enemies. They were composd of men of both political parties, each of whom aspired to be the political leader of El Paso. They were in full accord only in one aim—the political and personal ruin of W. W. Mills. The Republicans reasoned thus: "We cannot *lead* the Republican party until we down Mills." The Democrats reasoned thus: "We cannot *defeat* the Republican party until we down Mills!" They called themselves the "Anti-Mills Party."

In June, 1871, there appeared in all the Republican (radical) newspapers of Texas to which these parties could gain access a most slanderous and libelous publication against myself, purporting to be the resolutions of a Republican convention of El Paso County, declaring me to be of infamous character and "capable of all the crimes in the calendar."

This document was signed by three Americans as "President" and "Secretary" of the convention, and *purported* to be signed by fifteen of the most prominent Mexicans of the county, *all* of whom were my friends and *none* of whom had ever attended any such "convention."

I received written statements from *all* of these Mexican gentlemen declaring their friendship for me and denouncing the forgery of their names. This crime was severely punishable by the laws of Texas, and the punishment was double wherever the name of another person was used to give respectability to the libel, and I could have caused these men to have been arrested and carried to Austin and punished there, but now that so many years have elapsed and these vicious and guilty men have gone to their last account I do not regret that they escaped, and I omit their names.

Simultaneously with the publication of the libel mentioned above there appeared in all the accessible Democratic papers in the State a letter signed "Victor" (B. F. Williams), containing the same slanders but somewhat changed in form, showing concert of action.

Then Governor Hamilton wrote me a letter cautioning me against any resort to violence and bidding me bide my time.

Then our little boy sickened and died, and Mrs. Mills' health began to fail, and as my enemies, nearly all of whom had received substantial favors from me, showed no sign of relenting, we went again to Austin, this time in the mail coach, carrying the remains of our first born in the "boot," to be buried at the Capital of Texas, where we hope also to rest when life's fitful fever is past.

But neither then nor at any time did we intend to abandon our El Paso home.

Two years later the beautiful little Mary, our second and last child, died at Austin, and we laid her beside her brother. Then, indeed, our skies were gray.

A. J. FOUNTAIN—MY WORST ENEMY.

In 1869 there arose a bitter controversy between myself and A. J. Fountain, who had for several years been my special deputy in the customs house at El Paso, which controversy attracted great interest on this frontier, and even in Austin and Washington City. There was much angry correspondence and an official investigation, but as I came out of the contest unscathed I will content myself with publishing only one of Fountain's letters and "let it go at that."

El Paso, Texas, May 13, 1869.

W. W. Mills, Esq.:

My dear Sir—The conversation I had with you last evening left upon my mind the impression that you entertained a belief that I would oppose you and your friends, politically, should your choice for the Legislature in the coming contest fall upon some other person than myself, and that I would endeavor to secure to my support cliques and factions of our party, in this county, that are antagonistic to you, and that to do so, I would be compelled to give pledges which, if carried out, would result to your prejudice. If I am correct in my impression (and I hope I am not), I regret very much that our years of intimate acquaintance has made you know me only to doubt me.

I, therefore, desire to enter upon a full explanation of my feelings towards you, not for the purpose of trying to secure your support or influence in my behalf, but to disabuse your mind of any impression that you may have that under any circumstances, whatever, I would place myself in opposition to you. It is unnecessary for me to recapitulate the circumstances under which we first became associated as friends. I received from you a lucrative appointment, which I held some two years. It is not on account of pecuniary obligations that I feel myself in honor bound to stand your supporter to the last extremity. The year previous to my coming to El Paso to live I had been engaged in an enterprise which promised, if successful, a fortune. I had partners who advanced a small portion of the original capital invested, and who, when I was confined to my bed suffering for months from wounds received while risking my life to advance their interest as well as my own, not only robbed me of all I had, but slandered me to my friends to excuse their conduct. Weak and poor as I was, I made them such a fight that they were compelled to use the most despicable means to defeat me, and I endeavored to find employment to support my children; they, having the aid of men of influence who still were my friends and desired to assist me, poisoned them against me by villainous lies and slanderous misrepresentations of my conduct. They acknowledged that they endeavored to poison *your* mind against me when I had a prospect of again rising, and that if you had not stood my friend they would have succeeded in their threats of driving me from the country. It was then through your interposition that these parties failed, and that I have had the satisfaction of receiving humble apologies from some of them for the wrong they did me. I was taught in my youth never to allow an insult to pass unresented, never to forgive an enemy who deliberately injured me, never to be ungrateful to one who befriended me. I believe that you were my friend when I most needed one, *you shall never have cause to regret that act,* and I would consider myself as great a villain as the world contains, if *under any circumstances whatever,* I arraigned myself among the number of your enemies, personal or political; or if I should passively witness any attack upon your private or political character, and not strike a blow in your defense. Whatever bad qualities I may possess (and I know I have many faults) I am no *ingrate.* I consider myself bound to support you whenever you require that support, and will give you all the assistance in my power to enable you to accomplish any object you have in view, and if you are not entirely satisfied that all I do in this connection is to show my gratitude, I am indeed unfortunate and can only wait patiently for time to prove my sincerity.

Very respectfully,

A. J. FOUNTAIN.

The recent mysterious murder or disappearance of Fountain in New Mexico renders further comment from me improper, except to state that very soon after writing the above letter he became my bitter assailant and traducer, and *at the time he wrote the letter* he was secretly conspiring with my most unscrupulous and most relentless enemies. His malignity appeared to increase with the failure of every effort to do me harm.

ARREST AT SAN ELEZARIO—ASSAULT BY ATKINSON.

In 1871, when the Davis administration was in full power and the notorious State police of that day were "rough riding" over the State, one John Atkinson (of whom more anon) commanded that force in El Paso County.

I went, with my wife and brother, A. E. Mills, in my ambulance to attend court at San Elezario, which was then the county seat. There was a State law against carrying arms, "except when traveling," and we went armed. Immediately upon arriving at the county seat my brother and myself were arrested by Atkinson and his police and taken from the ambulance, leaving Mrs. Mills alone, and carried toward the jail. At that time the Mexican people thoroughly hated Atkinson and his party, but were devoted to me and my friends. There was some halting and parleying before we reached the jail door, and we saw groups of Mexicans consulting here and there and occasionally one with arms. I remember my brother whispering to me: "These people will take us out of jail before morning, but we will probably be dead."

A Mexican, Maximo Arranda, who was justice of the peace, summoned Atkinson to bring his prisoners before him, and immediately ordered our release upon the ground that we were travelers and had a right to carry arms.

That night I went alone and unarmed to the house of a respectable citizen, where I had been invited to a party. I took a seat at one side of the room. The District Judge, District Attorney, Sheriff and Clerk of the Court, all enemies of mine, were dancing. When all were seated and the music ceased Atkinson stood before me, one hand on his six-shooter and the other in my face, and called me many pet names, the mildest of which were "coward" and "liar," and threatened to shoot me if I spoke or moved.

I remained silent, and my assailant was called away. Presently Johnnie Hale sat down beside me and whispered that he had two pistols and would give me one if I would not use it unless attacked and would go away with him. I accepted, and we left the house.

Court was in session, and the next day the grand jury presented an indictment against Atkinson for aggravated assault. The District Attorney declined to prosecute, and James A. Zabriskie volunteered to take his place. Will the reader believe that that "carpet-bag" Judge (from Canada), appointed by Governor Davis to administer justice over a people he had never seen or heard of, forbade Zabriskie to prosecute for aggravated assault, and declared from the bench that he knew it was merely a simple assault *because he witnessed it himself!* I take pleasure in recording the fact that this Judge was removed from office by the Legislature of Texas. Atkinson's violent death is recorded in my account of the San Elezario mob, and that of Johnnie Hale in the account of the killing of Kramkrauer, Campbell, Hale and a Mexican at El Paso in 1881.

FROM EL PASO TO AUSTIN—STAGE DRIVERS.

In February, 1872, we went in the stage coach from El Paso to Austin. The party consisted of Mrs. Mills, myself, Charles H. Howard and a young St. Louis lawyer named Bowman, who was taking his first lessons in frontier life and customs.

If I desired to learn any man's true character I would want to take a long day and night journey with him in a stage coach. Want of sleep and other annoyances, vexations and privations bring out at times all the ill-nature and selfishness one may possess; and, again, when everything goes smoothly and all are moving leisurely and silently over some long stretch of prairie or plain and the weather is pleasant, men appear to cast all cares and reserve to the wind and converse with each other more frankly and confidentially than elsewhere. At least, that has been my experience and observation.

Here and during other like experiences Mrs. Mills made the acquaintance of the stage driver, a character difficult to describe and now almost extinct.

He possessed the courage of the soldier and something more. The private soldier goes where he is told to march, and fights when he is ordered, but he has little anxiety or responsibility; but the stage driver in those times had to be as alert and thoughtful as a General. There was not only his duty to his employers but his responsibility for the mails (he was a sworn officer of the Government), but the lives of the passengers often depended upon his knowledge of the country and of the Indian character, and his quick and correct judgment as to what to do in emergencies. Like the sailor, he was something of a fatalist, but he believed in using all possible means to protect himself and those under his charge.

Your stage driver was usually of a serious, almost sad disposition; inclined to be reticent, particularly about himself and his former life, and his surname was seldom mentioned by himself or his associates. He was known as "Bill" or "Dave" or "Bobo" or "Buckskin," or some such sobriquet. When, however, he could be induced to talk about himself as a stage driver his stories were always interesting and sometimes thrilling. There was occasionally a liar among them, but most of them had really experienced such serious adventures and "hair-breadth scapes" that it was not necessary for them to draw upon their imaginations.

Rough, profane and unclean of speech among their own sex, they were remarkably courteous to lady passengers and ever thoughtful of their comfort and feelings, and more than once, on arriving at a station where the drivers were to be changed, I have heard one whisper to another: "Remember, Sandy, there is a little lady in the coach." This was sufficient.

During the most interesting portion of this trip we had two drivers, "Uncle Billy," who was going to San Antonio on leave, and "Bobo," the regular driver. They vied with each other in trying to make everything pleasant for Mrs. Mills. They would prepare the high driver's seat with cushions and blankets and assist her to mount it, and for hours would call her attention to points of interest or entertain her with stories of their experiences, humorous or tragic.

One morning just after daybreak Bobo halted the coach and said: "Gentlemen, get your guns ready; the prints of moccasined feet here are as thick as turkey tracks."

And so it was, and the tracks were fresh. A large party of Indians had very recently crossed the road, but we saw nor heard more about them.

At "Head of Concho" we came upon a herd of buffalo, and, of course, we dismounted and wantonly fired into them, with what effect I do not know, except that some one wounded an immense bull so seriously that he became angry or sullen and refused to run away as the others did. We, with our deadly Winchesters, ceased firing at him, as he was of no use to us, but not so with the young St. Louis lawyer. He wanted to do something that he could tell about at home, and so he advanced upon the irate animal with his little thirty-two calibre pistol, firing as he went. He was encouraged and animated by the shouts of Bobo and Uncle Billy: "Charge him, mister," "You've got him," "The next shot will fetch him," etc.

Mrs. Mills said: "Why, Uncle Billy, that animal will kill the man! Call him back!" Uncle Billy said: "Why, *of course,* he'll kill him. Now you just watch, and you'll see fine fun. He'll toss that little lawyer higher'n the top of this coach." And yet Uncle Billy and Bobo were not cruel men.

SOME TEXAS LAWYERS.

In 1871 I held a judgment for $50,000 which I had obtained in the El Paso District Court against a citizen of El Paso County for having caused my arrest and imprisonment by the Confederates in 1861, as related in my war story. This judgment being in full force and I being in Austin, my friend, Major De Normandie, then Clerk of the Supreme Court, introduced me to a prominent attorney of De Witt County, Texas, who informed me that the defendant owned property in De Witt County out of which my judgment, or a large portion of it, could be satisfied. I implored this attorney to act for me in De Witt County, and on my return home I sent him, at his request, a certified copy of the judgment and received a letter from him dated June 7th, 1871, informing me that they had written out a levy which they would proceed with in a day or two, and requesting me to send them some money for costs, which I did. After long delay I wrote this attorney, asking to be informed of the result, and he replied that the whole proceeding was a failure because he had dated the levy *on a Sunday,* which mistake vitiated the whole proceeding and that my rights were lost.

He stated that "strange as it might seem" he had been led to make the mistake by an error in an almanac in his office. As this attorney did not suggest any remedy for his own blunder or institute any further proceeding I concluded then, and believe now, that political prejudice or some other unworthy motive had influenced him to act in bad faith with his client. The attorney and the defendant were both Confederates and Democrats, while I was a Union man and a Republican, and much bitter feeling had grown out of the suit and the acts preceding and attending it.

I met this lawyer in Austin a year or so later, and he made no further explanation except to affirm that it "made no difference, because the Supreme Court had decided that my judgment was void." As a matter of fact, and of record, the Supreme Court had decided that the judgment was valid. And here I will state a fact which I hope the reader will remember when he comes to read the case following this one—*this gentleman was later on elected a Judge of the Supreme Court of Texas.*

My judgment for $50,000 (mentioned in the preceding paragraphs) was in 1868, before the Supreme Court at Austin on writ of error or appeal, or both, taken or claimed to have been taken from the District Court of El Paso County by the defendant. A supersedeas bond for one hundred thousand dollars *damages,* signed by John Hancock and Thomas J. Divine, was filed with the Clerk of the Supreme Court by the appellant's attorney, whom I will not name here.

When this appeal came on for trial my attorney discovered to his amazement that the words "thousand" and "damages" had been erased on the face of the bond and the words "costs" inserted instead of the word damages.

It is proper to explain to the non-professional reader that this fraud and forgery changed the nature of the bond, so that if I gained the case—and I *did* gain it—I could recover from the sureties, who were both wealthy men, only one hundred dollars "*costs,*" instead of the full amount of the judgment, namely, fifty thousand dollars "*damages.*" The Judges were, of course, astounded, and called the Clerk, Major de Normandie, who being sworn testified that the record had been borrowed by appellant's attorney when it was in its original condition, and that when it was returned the erasures and forgery were in the handwriting of said attorney. The guilty attorney was present, but stood mute, offering no explanation or excuse for his acts. The Court, at some length and with strong indignation, rendered its decision dismissing the appeal and leaving my judgment in full force, but the wrong to me had been done, so far as the bond was concerned.

My loss was about forty thousand dollars.

If any one questions any of the above statements he will find abundant proof in the Reports of the Supreme Court of Texas:

Hart vs. Mills, 31st Texas, page 304, and Hart vs. Mills, 38th Texas, pages 513 and 517.

This thing was not done in a corner. Every attorney of that Court knew the facts exactly as I have stated them, and it was a duty they owed to themselves and to the profession to have disbarred the attorney, but he stood fairly well socially and had been a "good" Confederate and Democrat and I was only a frontiersman and Republican, and so *they elected him a Judge of the Supreme Court of Texas,* as had been done with the lawyer in the case mentioned above. I believe there is a legal maxim, or a legal axiom, or a legal *fiction,* that there can be no wrong without a remedy, and I am asked why I did not pursue the remedy. Oh, I don't know. I suppose every man of affairs has sometimes in his life done or neglected things which he could scarcely explain afterward, even to himself. I was seven hundred miles away, and my attorney was well paid in advance for looking out for my interests, and unless he choose to act I don't think I could have broken the combination. There are times when even the most energetic men become discouraged and weary of strife, and for a time at least feel like letting things drift as they may.

In 1873 I had a suit pending in court at El Paso involving the title to valuable real estate, and I paid an El Paso attorney $800 to attend to it.

In my absence and without my consent this lawyer compromised me out of court for a worthless consideration, and I lost the property. Of course, I might have repudiated this compromise, but I was handicapped by the fact that the property in question was held in trust for me by my brother, E. A. Mills, and the lawyer had induced him, by claiming to have authority from me, to re-convey the property; and the legal machinery here at that time was such that I thought it hopeless to litigate further.

LITIGATION ABOUT EL PASO PROPERTY.

When the Confederate forces left El Paso and the United States troops took possession, in 1863, such of the county records as had been preserved from destruction were by common consent delivered to me for safe keeping, to be turned over to the proper county officers as soon as such officers should be appointed or elected. This, and my long residence here, gave me the opportunity of becoming the best informed man in El Paso as to titles, boundaries, possession, etc., so that when the railroads and the boom came and city lots became valuable and there was a general shaking up and deciding of titles by many suits in the courts, I was almost a standing witness. I verily believe that more of these cases were decided upon my testimony than on that of any other half dozen witnesses, and all this testimony was given without receiving or expecting a dollar's compensation. The juries believed me, and so far as I know not even the most zealous lawyer ever questioned my testimony, though there were some "keen encounters of wits."

In one instance I saved to a certain litigant property on El Paso street now worth fifty thousand dollars simply by producing an ancient deed which I had had in my possession for twenty-five years and had forgotten. The book, "Record of Deeds," had been destroyed, but the acknowledgment of the vendor was on the deed itself, and the suit was withdrawn.

I believe that in the main these cases were decided according to law, which was the best that could be done;

but if, as we are told, there are certain eternal principles of right and justice, higher than those men make for their own convenience, then surely these principles were sometimes violated, for deserving men lost property which by such principles should have been their's by such trivial neglect as failing to record a deed or to pay taxes or to preserve evidence of occupancy, or some other fact, or worse still, by false testimony.

CONFISCATION—AN EXPLANATION—NOT AN APOLOGY.

All Governments, including the Southern Confederacy, have written in their statute books that whoever engages in rebellion or takes up arms against their authority shall forfeit not only his property but his life.

I am glad now that my Government did not enforce these harsh penalties against any of the Confederates.

In 1864 the United States District Judge for New Mexico, himself a Southern man, held that his Court had the power to libel and confiscate the real estate of such citizens of El Paso County, Texas, as were then in arms against the United States. He based this claim upon an Act of Congress approved March 3d, 1863, which provided that "The jurisdiction of the United States Court for New Mexico is hereby extended over the citizens of El Paso County only in cases not instituted by indictment."

I, being Collector of Customs, had caused this act to be passed to enable me to condemn and sell goods smuggled into El Paso County (there being then no United States Courts in Texas). I am frank to say that I did not then even dream of the confiscation of any one's real estate.

The United States Attorney and Marshal for New Mexico came to El Paso and libeled the property of certain leading Confederates and proceeded against it in the United States Court at Mesilla, New Mexico, and certain of these lands and lots were declared forfeited and were sold at El Paso by the United States Marshal, and I purchased a portion of this property, as did others. I paid the Marshal eighteen hundred dollars good and lawful money therefor, and received and recorded his deeds.

I protected the property of some of my Confederate neighbors, Dowell's and Stephenson's and others.

Along with what I purchased was a six-eighths' interest in the El Paso town tract belonging to the Gillett brothers, who were then absent with the Confederate army; but some years later, when they returned to El Paso and we patched up a peace, I proposed to them that if they would join their title with mine I would pay their debts, amounting to a few thousand dollars, which debts were a lien on the property, and we would hold it share and share alike.

This they declined to do, and in the end they lost it all. So did I, for years later the Supreme Court of the United States decided, *not* that the property was not subject to forfeiture, as all such property certainly was, but simply that the Act of Congress referred to did not confer the jurisdiction claimed by the Court at Mesilla.

Without a murmur I reconveyed all the property to the original owners and lost the eighteen hundred I had paid the Marshal.

Then the Gillett's creditors sold them out. I had held possession of the town tract and paid taxes on it for five years.

It has been said that I purchased the property of Simon Hart at the confiscation sale. That is not true.

I purchased that property at Sheriff's sale on a judgment for false imprisonment, which I obtained against Hart in a Texas court, which judgment was twice affirmed by the Supreme Court of Texas.

In 1871 I was the owner of a portion of Franklin Heights, of the city of El Paso, then known as Hart Survey, No. 9.

Being in Washington City I met my friend, Gen. Robert B. Mitchell, and gave him a power of attorney to sell the property. He sold to different purchasers, to the amount of $14,000, and we divided the proceeds share and share alike.

The property was then considered valueless by those who knew less than we did, but it is now worth forty-fold what we received for it. Among the purchasers were George W. Gray of Washington City and one Peck of Kansas, and others.

The recording of the deeds in El Paso County aroused the jealousy and hatred of my El Paso enemies, and, heedless of what harm they might do to others so long as there was a prospect of injuring me, they wrote the purchasers that I had no title to Survey No. 9, that the property was worthless, and that I was a swindler.

It is strange that the purchasers took these statements at par, and instead of investigating or communicating with me they sued me in Washington City for the purchase money, charging fraud, and got service on me there. I demurred them out of court, and came home, and being angry with the purchasers I paid no further attention to them or their troubles.

None of them ever asserted their rights to the property, WHICH THEY COULD HAVE DONE SUCCESSFULLY IF IN TIME.

These strange facts being of record in El Paso County have caused a lot of talk, and many a lawyer has believed he had made an important discovery and has had visions of profitable litigation. I have been interviewed about this transaction one hundred times, more or less.

"STAR" MAIL CONTRACTS—THE FIRST TRUST—1869-70.

After the war I and my El Paso friends became involved in a bitter contest with the San Antonio and El Paso Mail Company, which continued for several years. At that time the great lines of railroads were reaching out toward the west and southwest, and many mail routes, hundreds of miles in length, were preceding them. These mails were carried in stage coaches, buckboards and on horseback. Millions were expended annually by the Government for this service, and it was harvest time for the two wealthy companies who monopolized the larger routes, the above named company in Texas and another company in the northwest.

This Texas company failed year after year to deliver the mails at El Paso according to their contract, and our people were practically without mail facilities, which was a great privation, and the people complained to the Post Office Department but without avail, because the wealthy company had powerful influence with some of its high officials and a strong lobby in Washington City. Then the El Paso merchants and people held an indignation meeting, denounced the company and appointed Col. Jas. A. Zabriskie and myself to represent them at Washington, and after taking much testimony all along the line we went on our mission at our own expense.

After a careful investigation in Washington City, during which we found more rottenness than we had dreamed of, and in higher places than we had suspected, we secured a hearing before the joint committee of

Congress on Retrenchment, composed of seven Senators and fourteen Representatives and the contest began.

Zabriskie and Mills for the complainants, "the prosecution," and the distinguished Judge Pascal of Texas, and the still more distinguished Jere Black of Maryland for the Mail Company, "the defense." It was a "go as you please" contest. Three days were consumed in reading testimony, in quarreling and in arguments before that distinguished court or jury, and I flatter myself that we youths from the frontier held our own with these veterans of the Washington bar. (At least I am as proud of what I did there as the average young El Paso lawyer is when he wins a cow case against a railroad or makes a free silver speech.) I had recently been "suspended" as Collector at El Paso, and I charged that the Mail Company had employed Pearson & Williams at El Paso as scavengers to hunt for charges against me.

F. P. Sawyer, the principal man of the Mail Company, was present and took the stand and denied this charge, and stated that "out of consideration for others" he had tried to have me retained in office. On cross examination I led him to repeat these statements *most solemnly,* and then handed to Senator Patterson, the Chairman, the original of the following letter, which he read aloud to the committee:

"Washington, June 2d, 1869.

"W. M. Pearson, Esq., El Paso, Texas.

"Dear Sir: Yours of the 10th instant was this A. M. received and already placiet in Secretary Boutwell's hands to strengthen those already on file in his office which has as I suppose you have hird removed the greatest man in the U. S. as per his own opinion. I think this last affidavit of Mr. Wardwell's is a clincher. You have done your duty manfilly & have no doubt havedone that People of that western county a grat and lasting good. I have written you several letters to El Paso suppose you have them all. Yours very truly, (Signed) F. P. Sawyer."

The scene was somewhat dramatic. There was no attempt to deny the authenticity of the letter. I was not in a merciful mood. Never mind what I said. That millionaire perjurer left that committee room weeping like a child.

Colonel Zabriskie's speech before those potent, grave and reverend Señors was as fine a piece of oratory as one would wish to listen to. Our victory was complete. The unanimous report of the joint committee, dated April, 1870, is before me, but it is too long for publication here and I will condense it conscientiously. They say: "The committee find that in July, 1867, a contract was awarded to E. Bates for carrying a weekly mail between San Antonio and El Paso, Texas, seven hundred miles, for thirty-three thousand dollars a year; and they find that without warrant of law and without giving other bidders any opportunity to compete, this compensation was in eighteen months increased from $33,000 to $333,617! This was done by adding new routes, some of them longer than the original one and running at right angles to it and increasing the number of trips and 'expediting' the 'speed.' They say: 'Charges were made that the service was not perfectly performed and that the contractor had wholly failed to perform his contract, and there is no doubt in the minds of the committee that these charges were substantially true up to the latter part of 1868. It is also charged that that the Mail Company had sufficient influence with some of the postmasters to procure from them false certificates of the arrivals of the mails. The committee find that —— ———, postmaster at El Paso, Texas, certified that out of thirty-seven mails due at El Paso for a certain period, only ten ever arrived, and subsequently sent to the Department a certificate stating that all of the thirty-seven mails had arrived on time. For this and other reasons the committee recommend his dismissal. All the evidence concurs that the mails in Texas are so unsafe that no one dare trust money to them." The report says: "In making these increases of service and compensation the Postoffice Department seems to have given great weight to the representations of Judge Paschel, State Agent of Texas, probably not knowing that he was also the attorney of the Mail Company and himself interested in the contract." The report says: "It is evident that much feeling exists and powerful influences are interested both for and against the Mail Company." I know of no "powerful influence" *against* the Mail Company unless the committee refer to Zabriskie and myself, for we were alone in that contest.

Well, the result was a curtailment of the Mail Company's compensation by several hundred thousand dollars during the years for which they claimed the contracts, and a saving to the Government of an equai sum, and finally a return to something like fair and honest dealing in letting of such contracts.

While we were making our fight on the Mail Company of the Southwest, as above related, Col. Joe McCibbin was attacking a company who had by the same means monopolized the main routes in the Northwest, and he was trying to expose their frauds. Though acting independently, we sympathized and sometimes consulted with each other, and became fast friends. McCibbin was a man of fine ability, had been a member of Congress from California and in 1856 had been the second to Senator David C. Broderick of that State in the duel with Judge David S. Terry, in which the brilliant Senator was killed. McCibbin bore a striking resemblance to and in his manner was much like my friend, the elder Dr. Samaniego of Juarez. His fight was not concluded when we left Washington, and on my return a year or two later I asked him how it had terminated. He replied: "Oh, I am on the inside. I am the attorney for the Mail Company and am well paid for my services. You and Zabriskie had better get in. You can easily do so, and it don't pay to fight other people's battles. You get neither money nor thanks."

McCibbin then told me that the Mail Company had paid him $20,000 in cash to stop the fight, and were then paying him $10,000 per year as their Washington attorney. I would not state what McCibbin told me had he not later on made the same statement under oath to a committee of Congress and boldly defended his conduct. Did he do wrong? I don't know. His was a free lance. I sometimes envy the happy ignorance of those who tell me that they always know exactly what is right and wrong.

Yes, Zabriskie and I could have "got in," but we did not.

VICTORIO, THE GREAT APACHE GENERAL.

I could fill a book larger than the one I am writing with true stories of Indian raids and fights and massacres and captivities on this frontier, but I refrain.

In my war story I gave an account of one of the most desperate fights, where one who was kin of mine died, fighting bravely but hopelessly, and I will briefly mention here that final "round up" of the hostile savages of this section, the capture of Victorio and his band by the combined troops of our country and Mexico, within forty miles of El Paso, just twenty years ago. I give here an extract from a letter I wrote from El Paso to Mrs. Mills at Austin, dated September 24th, 1880, as follows: "If I had of late jumbled my accounts of Indians and war and politics and killings and adventures and anecdotes all into one letter I might have written one that would have interested all the good people at Fair Oaks, 'Chicos y Grandes.' I wrote you from Fort Davis that the Indians were gone. They were gone to the Candelerio Mountains, forty miles south of Quitman, and they are there yet. Since then they have stolen two herds of cattle from Dr. Samaniego, fifty miles from El Paso, killing the herders. Yesterday a small band crossed the river at the Canutilla, sixteen miles above here. Three days ago our troops and friendly Indians crossed here into the land of God and Liberty to concentrate with other forces who crossed below and above, to make a combined attack on Victorio *today*. But the wiley chief may not be there. Considering the number of his braves, he is the greatest commander, white or red, who ever roamed these plains. For more than a year he has out-manoeuvered our officers with six times his number and all the appurtenances of war, and when he has not out-generaled them he has *whipped them.* In sober truth, he is the veriest devil 'that ere clutched fingers in a captive's hair.' "

(I regret that neither at the War Department at Washington nor elsewhere have I been able to obtain an official account of the defeat of Victorio's band. The fight took place at Tres Castillas, southeast of El Paso. Only the Mexican soldiers happened to be in at the death, although our troops rendered valuable assistance on both sides of the boundary line in getting Victorio into a position where he was forced to fight either our troops or the Mexicans. Victorio and a hundred warriors were killed on the field and as many Indians were made prisoners. Col. Juaquin Terrazas of Chihuahua, a brave and skillful Indian fighter, commanded the Mexican troops.)

THE KILLING OF CLARKE AND WILLIAMS—THE CAUSES—1870.

On a fine autumn day, thirty years ago, on El Paso street, where the Mundy Block now stands, Gaylord J. Clarke and B. F. Williams were shot to death within a few moments of each other and within a few feet of each other.

In order that the reader may understand the causes which led up to these tragedies I will give a brief sketch of the career of each of the four men most directly connected with the quarrel or quarrels and their relation to each other and to the writer. Clarke was a New York man who had been my college chum, and the most intimate friend of my early manhood. At the age of twenty-four he was elected to a *State* office in New York. Later he had gone to Nebraska in the hope of some day representing that *State* in the United States Senate. In 1867 he wrote me that he had failed in everything and was destitute. I sent him the means to come to El Paso, gave him an appointment in the Customs House, and later I sent for his wife and child. Clarke was a scholar, a lawyer and at the time of his death was Judge of the El Paso District. He was a Republican.

B. F. Williams came to El Paso about the time that Clarke came. He was also a lawyer, had served in the Confederate army and was a Democrat.

Albert H. French was a Boston man, who had gone to California in his youth and had come to El Paso in 1863 as a Captain of California Volunteers, had married there and was a peace officer of the county.

A. J. Fountain has been mentioned elsewhere in these pages.

The quarrels grew out of an election held about a year previous, in which Clarke and French supported Hamilton for Governor and myself for the Legislature; Fountain and Williams leading the opposition. The county seat was at San Elizario, and the whole county voted there, the election lasting four days, and was held under military supervision. I here show what occurred. Judge French wrote me:

"After the battle, December 4th, 1869.

"Dear Mills: We won the election, but the first night, we having one hundred and forty-three to their forty-eight votes, they opened the box and scratched our one hundred and forty-three votes for themselves. Fountain's name represents yours on the scratched tickets. I have sworn two hundred and seventy-seven men who voted for you. You got only one hundred and thirty-four as counted. Yours, French."

(French was at the time County Judge.)

Clarke wrote me from El Paso, I being at Austin assisting in the management of Hamilton's campaign:

"Whole number of Hamilton tickets polled, two hundred and seventy-three; number as declared by registrars, one hundred and twenty-two. A majority of our tickets were scratched clear through and changed to Davis candidates. As ever yours,

Gaylord J. Clarke."

Lieutenant Verney, who presided over this election, was for other offences dismissed from the army a few years later. Our Legislative District, which had three Representatives, was comprised of a dozen counties and extended from El Paso to the Gulf of Mexico. Col. Nelson Plato of Brownsville and myself were running as Independent Republicans on the Hamilton ticket, and were fairly elected by the people, but the fraud in El Paso County and other places defeated us and gave the seats to those called "Regular Republicans."

Davis was inaugurated Governor and Fountain was all powerful at the State Capital.

But now trouble began for the victors. Williams believed that by supporting Davis and Fountain and aiding to defeat and otherwise injure me he had earned the Judgeship of the El Paso District, which was at the disposal of Fountain. But Fountain, always inexplicable, had other plans. He conceived an idea that it would be a good move to placate at least one gentleman and at the same time win away from me my friend, and so, to the surprise of everybody, he tendered the Judgeship to Clarke, and it was accepted.

It has been falsely stated that Clarke forsook me for office, but I quote here a brief note from him, written to me *after* he became Judge:

"Dear William: There are some things I would give much to talk to you about, but dare not write. They concern me closely and you, so far as regards your interests in this valley, but I defer them. When will you return home? Direct your letters for me *under cover* to D. C. B., Fort Davis. As ever yours, Gaylord."

The directing of letters "under cover" to mutual friends was to prevent their being stolen by the El Paso postmaster, who was of the Fountain faction.

Williams, by no means a well-balanced man, became furious and desperate at what he claimed to be, and what probably was, bad faith. He was particularly bitter toward Fountain and Clarke. He drank deeply and threatened terribly, and in his ravings declared that he had helped to "down" a better man than either of them.

In this state of mind on the day mentioned Williams went into Dowell's saloon and fired a pistol shot at close range at Fountain's left breast. Fountain's life was saved by his watch and his legs. He ran to Judge Clarke's house and asked protection and demanded that Williams be immediately arrested. Clarke was a firm believer in "the majesty of the law." He summoned a posse, consisting of E. A. Mills, John Evans, Johnnie Hale, John Gillett and J. A. Zabriskie, the District Attorney, and went to Williams quarters where Williams, being inside, had locked and bolted all the doors. French was there as a policeman. He went to the rear of the house to prevent Williams from escaping that way. Admittance being refused, the posse commenced to batter down the door. Then Williams came out, bare-headed, and leveled his shotgun at Judge Clarke, who stood very near. Clarke did not move, but said two or three times: "Don't you dare, Williams! Don't you dare!" Williams fired and Clarke staggered a few steps toward his home, then fell and died in a few moments without speaking. French, hearing the shot, came immediately upon the scene, and finding Williams still armed and running *"amuck,"* shot him twice with his pistol, and Williams died in about an hour.

THE CARDIS-HOWARD FEUD—THE MOB AT SAN ELEZARIO, 1877.

In 1877 but before the coming of the first railroad to El Paso and when the population had increased but little beyond what it was in the "sixties," there arose a bitter feud between two remarkable men, Lewis Cardis and Charles H. Howard, which resulted in the killing of both leaders and many other tragedies and agitated the people of the valley as nothing else ever did before or since.

Out of this local trouble evil-minded persons sought to manufacture excitement in Texas and throughout the country about a "war of races," "organized invasion from Mexico," and to involve the two countries in war. Cardis was an Italian who had served as an officer in Garibaldi's army in his youth, and had resided for several years at El Paso as a merchant and contractor, and knew the Spanish language and the Mexican character perfectly. He had been my lieutenant in political affairs during the sixties and early in the seventies he had, with my consent, succeeded me as the friend, adviser and leader of the Mexican people of the valley but was not so successful with the Americans.

Howard had come later from Texas. He was a lawyer and had served in the Confederate army. He was a man of imposing appearance, powerful physique and wonderful determination and courage, or rather recklessness. A friend of mine recently told me that the first time he saw Howard, although he knew nothing about him, *he feared him*. Howard's chief characteristic was *force;* that of Cardis was persuasion and management—a natural diplomat. Howard was a Democrat, Cardis was a Republican.

I was absent at the Capital of the State during the tragic month of which I am writing, but I knew both the parties well and was well informed of the nature of their quarrels. I had been intimate with Cardis for several years at El Paso. Howard had been my attorney, and I and my wife had once made the journey of eight days and nights from El Paso to Austin with him in the stage coach and he and I had returned to El Paso together in the same way. Besides, during several months preceding the tragedies each of them wrote me several letters complaining of the other, and each invoking my influence with the other. I still retain these letters, and I have before me as I write all the testimony taken by a United States Commission, consisting of Colonels King and Lewis of the regular army, which was appointed to investigate and report upon the *emente.* Howard had located some salt lakes about one hundred miles northeast of El Paso, from which (being on public land) the Mexicans had for many years taken salt free of cost. They were indignant at his action, and some of them threatened to take salt as before, but so far none of them had committed any lawless act. Howard, having influence with the county officials, caused the arrest and imprisonment of two prominent Mexicans at San Elezario for these threats. This was September 10th, 1877. A party of forty or fifty armed Mexicans at San Elezario forcibly released their two countrymen, and in turn arrested Howard and the County Judge, and organizing a Court of their own tried them for wrongs (real or supposed) done to them and their American friends, and possibly might have dealt severely with them had it not been for the intercession of Louis Cardis and the Parish Priest. As it was they extorted from him a promise and bond that he would leave the county never to return. Of course, this was lawlessness, but no more so than defrauding people of an election fairly won, or many other things which are common. Howard then went to New Mexico and "fired the Texas heart" with many telegrams about lawless work, war of races, invasion from Mexico, etc., etc. He charged that Cardis was the chief conspirator and marplot who had created all the trouble and had sought to have him (Howard) assassinated.

Howard called on Governor Hubbard for protection. There was great excitement throughout the State. Howard returned to El Paso and on the 10th of October, 1877, while Louis Cardis was writing a letter in the store of Joseph Schutz, Howard walked in with a shotgun and immediately shot him dead.

Now comes the most strange and pathetic part of this story. The people of San Elezario were threatening to kill Howard if he returned to that village, and the letter which Cardis had just finished and placed in his breast pocket was written to the leaders of that people pleading with them to refrain from all violence toward Howard and all others. This letter was bespattered with Cardis' blood! I print the letter below, together with some extracts from Cardis' diary for the few days preceding his death, and also an affidavit of Adolph Krakaner, an eye-witness of the assassination:

"El Paso, Texas, October 10th, 1877.

"Friend Cipriano: The notice having been circulated by telegraph and in the newspapers that our county had risen against the Government and that the same had been invaded by armed people of the Republic of Mexico, General Hatch, commander of troops on this frontier, sent Lieutenant Rucker to investigate whether or not it is true that the property of the United States and the lives of the citizens of the United States are in danger on account of the afore-mentioned invasion, but the lieutenant nor his soldiers have neither the orders nor the wish to molest the citizens of this county, except to investigate the case and make his report to the General.

"The false notices that are in circulation are not worth anything, if the people will continue to do as advised by their friends. Tranquillity and peace and the truth will manifest itself in time. * * * Your friend, in haste, (Signed) Louis Cardis.

"P. S.—Do not pay any attention to the slanders that you hear against me, and my life. Let the people remain tranquil and we will get justice, and this is what we wish and need no more. L. C."

A true copy. (Signed) John S. Lond,
First Lieutenant and Adjutant Ninth Cavalry, Acting
Assistant Adjutant General.

(Extract from the diary of Louis Cardis, found on his body after his death at the hands of Howard. The diary is pierced through and through with buckshot.)

"October 1st, P. M.—Was told by Mr. Lujan that Juarez had been incarcerated by order of G. M. Garcia for having said he intended to go to the salt lakes, and that warrants for his (Lyjan's) arrest had been issued, and for the arrest of four others.

"October 2.—J. R. Mariani informed me that the people took up arms, arrested G. M. Garcia and Howard, and asked me to go to San Elezario and use my influence to pacify the excited people, which I did. Found the people very much excited against Howard only. I begged for his life with all my might and left San Elezario at about 3 o'clock A. M. on 3d after being satisfied that the people had taken my advice to let Howard and all the rest free. Arrived at El Paso 9 A. M. after twenty-six hours of no rest or sleep. On the 4th, at night, Howard arrived here at El Paso escorted by eight of the people, and on the 5th A. M. Howard left (I am told) for New Mexico."

AFFIDAVIT OF ADOLPH KRAKANER.

"I am the bookkeeper of S. Schutz & Bro., merchants at El Paso, Texas, who are also agents of the Texas and California Stage Company, of which Louis Cardis, deceased, was a sub-contractor, running the U. S. mail between this point and Fort Davis, Texas; hence Cardis had more or less transactions with the firm and came frequently into the store and office. On Wednesday, the 10th day of October, 1877, between 2 and 3 o'clock P. M., Louis Cardis, deceased, came into the office, requesting me to write a letter, which he wished to send down to Ysleta and San Elezario. He (Cardis) took a seat in a rocking chair standing near by, with his back turned toward the store door—the main entrance of the establishment. While I was writing the letter, which occupied my whole attention, Judge Charles H. Howard came into the store, and when Mr. Jos. Schutz, a member of the firm of S. Schutz & Bro., who was sitting at a little table in the office, saw Howard, who had a double-barreled shotgun in his hand, he left his seat and walked up toward Howard, saluting him in a loud voice, thus: "How do you do, Judge Howard?" This salute caught the attention of Cardis, who was yet seated in the rocking chair, and he turned his face toward the store door. He (Cardis) seeing Howard, left the chair, passed behind me (I was sitting at the desk writing), and took a position behind the high office desk. Mr. Schutz, seeing Howard raise his gun, in a harsh and exciting tone exclaimed: "Krakaner, come away from there!" I at once dropped the pen, got up from the office chair and was by no means slow in trying to reach the door. While I passed the place where Mr. Schutz stood I heard the latter say: "Don't shoot here, Judge; respect my house and my family." The moment I reached the door I heard the discharge of a gun and another one following in quick succession. Howard left the store at once, walking slowly down the street toward his house. When I went back into the office I found Cardis lying dead at the same place (behind the high desk), where I left him a few seconds previously alive. The desk behind which Cardis sought protection did only cover the upper part of his body; from the navel down to his feet his body was exposed to Howard. The latter, standing behind a showcase about forty feet from the place where Cardis stood, fired the first shot under the desk, the balls (buckshot) taking effect in the abdomen; Cardis then staggered, exposed his breast and received Howard's second shot in the heart.

"The time elapsed between my leaving the desk and the firing of the first shot was but a few seconds. There was not a word spoken between Howard and Cardis. When Cardis' body was removed from the place where he fell his pistol was found in the scabbard and was cocked.

"I omitted to state that to my knowledge Howard had not been in the store for a period of about nine months prior to this shooting affray.

"El Paso, Texas, January 31st, 1878.

"A. Krakaner."

Howard again fled to New Mexico, and on October 25th wrote the Governor again about the terrible "mob" in El Paso County, the peril of all Americans, and closed by saying: "If the Governor don't help us I am going to bushwhacking." He forgot that during the whole trouble he had been the only man who had shed any blood.

Howard returned to El Paso early in December. Lieut. John B. Tays was then in command of about twenty State troops (Rangers) then in El Paso County. Tays was a foreigner, an alien and a bitter partisan. I quote the opening lines of Tays' report of the bloody tragedies which followed, in order that the reader may have some idea of the lieutenant's conception of his duty. He says: "By request of Mr. Howard I sent an escort to El Paso on the 13th inst., as he wished to come to San Elezario on business. He rode down to San Elezario in the ranks." If "all Americans" were in danger, why was one man *only* selected to be protected by the Rangers?

Howard had tempted fate too far, and his day had come. But the bloody sequel shall be told in the language of another. Capt. Thos. Blair of the United States army, was on the ground with a detachment of regular soldiers, but to "interfere in the domestic affairs of a sovereign State" would offend the political sensibilities of many.

(President Cleveland was later on repudiated by his party for interfering with the pastime of a mob at Chicago.)

True, Governor Hubbard had had the good sense to call on President Hayes for assistance, and it had been granted, but unfortunately the order had not yet reached the Captain. Captain Blair, in his official report, says:

"As soon as Howard arrived in San Elezario the town was surrounded by a cordon of armed men (Mexicans) and pickets posted on all roads. As soon as Tays saw the state of affairs he and his party retreated to their quarters (which was a detached building with corral) and barricaded the doors and windows and cut port-holes in the walls. On Thursday morning the firing began, and continued with but few intermissions until the Rangers surrendered on Monday forenoon. Mr. Ellis, a merchant, was the first one killed; that was on Wednesday night. When the tumult began he went out to find out what it was, and not stopping when halted by one of their sentinels, was shot. Afterward his throat was cut and his body thrown into a acequia. On Thursday morning Sergeant Mortimer, of the Rangers, was killed while making his way to the building where the others were posted. The Rangers consisted of just twenty men, I believe. With them in the building were Howard and his colored servant, Mr. Atkinson, a merchant of San Elezario, a Mr. Loomis from Fort Stockton, I believe, and Mrs. Campbell, the wife of one of the Rangers, and her two children. After hearing that I had been inside Mrs. Marsh and Mrs. Campbell went down from El Paso on Sunday morning. Mrs. Marsh got out her son, who was with the Rangers, but the Mexicans disarmed him and retained him prisoner. Mrs. Campbell got out her daughter-in-law and her two children. The Ranger party on Monday found that they could not hold out much longer, the men were being overcome by sleep, and under a flag of truce went out and had a talk with the leaders, who told them if they would give up Howard it was all they wanted. This he refused to do. They then said that if Howard would come out he could soon make arrangements by which it would be all right. Tays returned and told him so, but told him also not to go unless he wanted to do so, that he would defend him to the last man. Howard returned with Lieutenant Tays to the leaders. However, after some talk they asked Tays to leave Howard to them and go into another room, which he refused to do, whereupon he was seized by about a dozen men and carried out and then found that all his party had surrendered at the instigation of Atkinson (it is said).

"During the afternoon Howard, Atkinson and McBride, Howard's agent, were all taken out and shot. A strong effort was made by the more violent of the party, and by those from the other side, to have all the Americans shot, but Chico Barela opposed this (it), said there had been enough blood shed, and that only after they had killed him could any more Americans be killed. Tuesday forenoon they were released, each one having his horse returned to him, but their arms were retained. Some of the Rangers with whom I have talked inform me they were all asked whether they were employed by the Governor of Texas or by Howard, and then each one was required to sign a blank paper. They were escorted as far as Sorocco by a guard.

"The mob is estimated by Lieutenant Tays at not less than five hundred, many of the leaders being from the other side. The loss was five Americans killed and at least one Mexican, belonging to a party under Captain Garcia, who tried to assist the Americans. The losses on the side of the mob are unknown, but at least five or six are known to have been killed and a large number, not less than forty or fifty, wounded."

During the siege Captain Blair held several conferences with the Mexican leaders, which he relates as follows:

"I found the people much excited over the fact that Howard, who had taken a life, was permitted to go at large, while two of their number who had only *said* that they would go for salt to his 'salinas' had been arrested, tried and sentenced to imprisonment. They said Howard had killed their friend Cardis, and they would have his life, cost what it might. I found their force to consist of about three hundred and fifty sober, well-organized, well-armed, determined men, with a definite purpose. Howard they wanted, nothing less, nothing else. I told them I thought they would regret their course, that for Howard personally I cared nothing, but I would be sorry if anything happened to Lieutenant Tays. Yes, they said, but why was he defending Howard?"

The object for which the Mexicans had armed and assembled being accomplished, they disbanded, seeking no more blood. They killed Howard because he had killed Cardis, their friend and leader. They had known Atkinson for fifteen years, and they killed him *on general principles.*

The killing of McBride was inexcusable murder. Ellis, the merchant, was, I believe, murdered by some personal enemy who took advantage of the turbulence to gratify private vengeance. Sergeant Mortimer, the only ranger who lost his life, was killed in the fight. Five were killed in all. All the other unfortunates were citizens who had exasperated the people by voluntarily attaching themselves to Howard's fortunes. There *were* some Mexicans, many or few, from the Mexican side of the river, who came as the commission report, "some to fight and some to steal," but there was no "organized invasion." Considerable property was taken or destroyed, but the *object* of the uprising was always clearly stated, and that object was *not* plunder.

The good feeling which has usually existed between the two races in the valley was soon restored, and no one has ever been punished for participation in this deplorable *emente*.

THE AFTER MATH.

It is not pleasant to have to write of what occurred after the mob had dispersed, and therefore I will be brief. The regular force of Rangers had behaved well and obeyed orders, but now Governor Hubbard ordered that an additional force should be recruited at Silver City, New Mexico, to assist the authorities and restore order in El Paso County. About thirty came. Of these the Judge Advocate General of the Army reviewing the testimony says:

"Many outrages were committed on innocent people in the neighborhood during the excitement, but of these not a few were perpetrated by members of the State force raised in New Mexico under authority of the Governor of Texas. These last seem especially to be responsible for the rapes, homicides and other crimes of which the people justly complain."

The United States Commissioners, Colonels King and Lewis, before whom all the testimony was given, say:

"On December 22d, another small force of about thirty men arrived from Silver City, who had been called into temporary service under telegraphic instructions from the Governor, but unhappily, as was natural and according to experience in raising volunteers along the border, when the exigencies of the occasion does not permit that delay which a wise discrimination in the choice of material would cause, the force of Rangers thus suddenly called together contained within its ranks an adventurous and lawless element, which, though not predominant, was yet strong enough to make its evil influence felt in deeds of violence and outrage matched only by the mob itself. Notable among these atrocities should be classed the shooting of two Mexican prisoners, who were bound with cords when turned over to the guard at Ysleta, ostensibly to bury the bodies of Howard, Atkinson and McBride, then lying in the fields of San Elizario, and when next seen, about an hour after, were pierced with bullet holes, their appearance giving rise to grave apprehension in unprejudiced minds that their death was 'neither necessary nor justifiable.' Another was the killing of the Mexican and the wounding of his wife in a house in Socorro, through the door of which a shot had, it was said, been fired, and, being a spent ball, had struck without hurting one of the Rangers belonging to Lieutenant Tays' company. On a personal examination by the board of all the outside doors of the house, there could be found no marks of a bullet-hole, but through an inner door, across the 'Sala,' behind which the unfortunate victim had received his death and his wife a serious wound, were counted no less than fifteen bullet-holes, piercing the door from the outside, and none merging from the inner side. These are regarded by the Board as wanton outrages."

These Rangers, like the leaders of the mob, escaped punishment.

THE BLOODY REIGN OF MARSHAL STUDEMEIER.

Twenty years ago, with the coming of the first railroads to El Paso, there came also many bad men, and our mayor and city fathers concluded in their wisdom that they must have a city marshal who would be "bader en anybody," and they succeeded beyond their most sanguine expectations. They imported one Dallas Studemeier, and installed him in that office.

His coming, if we can trace human events back to their causes, cost the lives of half a dozen men, his own included. The supplanted marshal, a Mr. Johnson, was the first victim. He was killed one night on San Antonio street, near its junction with El Paso, "by parties unknown," as was said at the time. No one dared ask why or by whom he was killed.

Studemeier brought with him a brother-in-law, one "Doc" Cummings, a man of his own ilk. Soon the Studemeier-Cummings party became involved in a quarrel with the four Manning brothers, who resided here at the time, and Cummings was killed by Jim Manning in a fight.

It is enough to say that Manning was fairly tried and acquitted on a plea of self-defense.

In the Bosquies above El Paso there were several parties of cowboys, both American and Mexican, some of whom were, no doubt, looking after their own cattle, while others were certainly looking after other people's cattle. One morning the bodies of two young Mexicans from Juarez were found dead at their camp near

Canutilla, sixteen miles above El Paso. They had been recently shot. The Mexicans of Juarez asked permission to send an armed party to take home the bodies, and they passed through El Paso. With them went a young German named Kramkauer, a stranger in El Paso, but who we afterward learned was a good man, and he certainly was a brave man.

On their return, this party of about thirty armed men halted on El Paso street, appearing angry but making no threats or hostile demonstrations, but Kramkauer did not hesitate when questioned to say that the signs at the Mexican's camp clearly showed that the two young Mexicans had been surprised while preparing their breakfast and assassinated. This was too much for the American cowboys and their friends who had collected on the street, and for a time I feared a conflict between them and the thirty armed Mexicans, which I knew would be a bloody affair, and therefore interceded to prevent it. But the Mexican party sullenly moved south on El Paso street, and halted when about half way to the river. Now the wrath of the American party was turned toward Kramkauer, who remained on El Paso street, near the head of San Antonio, and one Campbell, of whose history or character I know but little, but who appeared to be the spokesman of the party, called on Kramkauer to retract what he had said. Kramkauer quietly but firmly refused, saying that he had stated only the truth. I was standing near these two men, and was surprised at the low, protesting, almost pleading tone of voice in which they spoke to each other. Both were sober, both were brave. The marshal, Studemeier, was standing near me and them, but spoke no word. Others soon gathered about us, but the young German was without friends. I believe these two men might not have fought, but Johnnie Hale, who was intoxicated, called out: "Turn her loose, Campbell; damn 'em, turn her loose," and drew his pistol. Studemeier, who stood within four feet of Hale, shot him in the back of the head, and Hale fell and died in a few moments. Campbell and Kramkauer fired simultaneously at each other, both shots taking effect. Each fired several times. Campbell fell, and the German staggered to the wall, and, leaning against it with his smoking pistol still in his hand, said, "I will fight till I die," and he died soon. Campbell lingered till the next morning, and died.

A second shot fired by Studemeier accidentally killed a Mexican who happened to be passing down the street. I do not know who Studemeier was shooting at then, and I don't believe he knew himself. Less than ten seconds time passed between the first shot and the last one, but four men were killed! Two of the three participants in the above affray having killed each other, and Studemeier having killed two men "on the side," as it were, he became a hero with the rabble and a *terror* to the more thoughtful of the city officials, who sought to get rid of him. But it is sometimes easier to catch such a man than it is to let him go. I found a way.

I was deputy United States marshal at the time, and at the next meeting of the council I presented a telegram from the United States marshal of New Mexico, stating that Studemeier had accepted an appointment as his deputy, thereby vacating the office of city marshal, and the city council declared it vacant. An alderman immediately nominated Studemeier to succeed himself, and Alderman Hague nominated the writer of these pages. The vote stood four and four, and then the mayor, to the surprise of many, gave the casting vote to Studemeier! One night, soon after the above occurrences, I went to a public meeting at the old Central hotel, and in the hall, in the presence of many people, Studemeier accosted and cursed and threatened to kill me, and called on me to defend myself. I was unarmed, and so informed him. He then produced two pistols, and generously offered to loan me one, but I had seen that trick played before, and I told him that as he and I were not good friends I did not feel like accepting a favor from him, and he went away. I went home and armed myself and returned to the meeting and met Studemeier, but nothing more was said or done. This was the last time, so far as I know, when I have been in any great peril from my fellow men—unless from their tongues.

There are probably as many Davids as Goliaths, and this desperado was about to meet his David—and his death. Dr. Manning was small of stature, modest in deportment, devoted to his family and his profession, and as to fighting, his disposition is well described in the words of the old negro, "Mammy," in speaking of her old master. She said, "Colonel Purdue want no man to go about hunting for no fuss, but if anybody brought a fuss to him and laid it in his lap, he would nuss it and coddle it and try to keep it from ketchen cold."

Studemeier gathered his few followers about him and announced that he was going to meet the Mannings and make peace or "have it out."

The meeting was at the old stand, Uncle Ben. Dowell's saloon. A peace was patched up, and of course some drinks were taken, and then all left except the marshal and Dr. Manning. Suddenly Studemeier found some pretext for anger, and, drawing his pistol, suddenly fired at Manning's heart. The bullet missed its mark but wounded the doctor in one hand (the other hand had been crippled in a former fight), yet the little man grappled the large one with one hand and with the other drew his pistol, and in an instant the giant lay dying on the ground!

This shall be my last story of bloodshed. I was foreman of the jury which tried Dr. Manning, and he was rendered a verdict of not guilty without leaving the box.

LONGMEIER—A CLOSE CALL.

In the bad times soon after the coming of the first railroad, I returned to El Paso as deputy United States marshal, and encountered many strangers, and was called to the custom house to appraise some liquor which had been smuggied by one Longmeier. Although I had nothing to do with the seizure of the liquor, Longmeier thought I had, or else he thought it no harm to kill a deputy marshal, anyhow.

That night, while sitting at supper with my back to a window which opened on the common (which window had a hanging curtain), I heard the landlord call from the outside: "Mills, get your pistol; a man is going to kill you." The landlord, John Woods, colored (who was afterwards killed by a policeman), had found Longmeier crouched at the window, pistol in hand, trying to find an opening through the curtain, and when asked what he was doing, replied that he was going to kill the d—n deputy marshal.

Longmeier fled and went to Silver City, and was soon after killed by a man of his own class.

A HOLD UP.

Soon after the above incident, I went one night about 9 o'clock to call for my wife, who was visiting some friends near McGoffin's place. As I walked unarmed and with my overcoat thrown over my shoulder, I heard and saw a man walking suspiciously behind me, and determined to watch him, but as he followed a different street at a junction I dismissed him from my mind. Suddenly he sprang from the bushes about fifteen feet from the road, with a very large pistol directed at me, and the following dialogue ensued:

He—"Halt! Your money or your life."

I—"My friend, I haven't a damn cent."

He—"Er, er. Hold up your hands."

I did as requested.

He—"Ain't you got no jewelry nor nothin'?"

I—"I told you no."

He—"I believe you are a d—n liar."

I—"Aint it bad enough to be broke without being insulted about it?"

He—"I've a damn notion to kill you, any how."

I—"I am afraid you will. You don't intend to kill me, but that pistol is pointed right at me, and you are nervous and it might go off."

I positively saw that man move his pistol so that, had it been discharged, the bullet would have missed me by several feet. His voice quivered and I could see him tremble.

He—"Throw off that overcoat and step to one side."

I complied.

I—"When you take the coat please take the papers from the pocket and leave them in the road."

More conversation, and then:

He—"Pick up your coat and walk straight down the middle of the road; no bad breaks, now, or by —— I will kill you."

And though I was never a Populist, I walked that night down the "middle of the road."

One day I passed where two strange roughs were evidently critisizing some new comer who they thought was claiming honors which did not belong to him. I heard one of them say contemptuously: "Calls himself the Deadwood Kid! Why, he's no more the Deadwood Kid than I am. Why, the Deadwood Kid has killed half a dozen men, an' I don't believe that '*moke*' ever killed anybody!"

Early one morning I heard a saloonkeeper talking to his friend, evidently about some row he had had the day or night before. He said, "Well, no; I don't think I was too drunk. Well, I was just about like I am now; and if he had got the best of me I wouldn't have said a word. But my own opinion is, I would have gone through him p-r-o-p-e-r-l-y."

The next day after the notorious ex-convict and desperado, Wesley Harden, was killed on San Antonio street by a worse man than himself, who was a constable or something, people, though not sorry at Harden's taking off, were shocked at the manner of it, but feared to condemn the act, because no one knew who would be the next victim. I was passing along the street, and a merchant friend called to me and said, seriously and in a low tone of voice, "What do YOU think about this killing of Harden?" I placed my hand at the side of my mouth and whispered, "I'll tell you if you say nothing about it. I have just been down to the undertakers and I saw Harden, and I think—I think he's dead!" I believe my friend kept my secret.

Some years ago my friend, Mr. Park Pitman, now (1900) the efficient clerk of El Paso County, was a candidate for a county office on the Democratic ticket, and was the only candidate of his party defeated—possibly because he was the best man on that ticket. Soon thereafter, I was a candidate for a city office on the Republican ticket, and was the only Republican defeated (whether we voted for each other or not is nobody's business). Soon after my defeat, I met Pitman with a party of friends, and I said to him: "Let us mingle our tears." He replied, "I am writing a book which is to be entitled, 'Bleeding Inwardly.' I will compliment you with a copy."

On my return from Washington City, in 1897, my friend, Zack White, congratulated me upon my appointment as United States Consul at Chihuahua, Mexico, and I told him I had been surprised at receiving so many congratulations and that I believed most of them sincere. He replied, "They are *all* sincere. It's like this; half of the people of this town are your friends, and, like me, they are glad of your success, and the other half are glad because you are going away. *It's unanimous.*"

I think a man who makes an "even break" among the people of El Paso does fairly well, and I "let it go at that."

The North American Review, November, 1889.

THE UNION MEN OF THE SOUTH.

By W. W. Mills.

In every Southern State at the commencement of the rebellion there lived a class of men, prominent and influential in political and social life, whose patriotism, devotion to principle, wisdom and courage, trials and sufferings, have been scarcely touched upon by late writers upon the war and its causes and results. Most of them were then of mature years; all of them had been born and reared in the South and were slave-owners. Many of them were Democrats; none of them were then Republicans. Most of them were disappointed at the election of Mr. Lincoln, and feared that his administration and that of the Republican party, which they considered sectional and aggressive, would be unfriendly, if not actually hostile, to the welfare of their section, where their pride, interests, and sympathies were all centered. Many of their wives, mothers and daughters were Secessionists. Their sons, many of them, were the first to enlist in the Confederate ranks. These men doubted the policy of secession, and, with a courage and manhood which have no parallel, denounced the movement and predicted its failure and the ruin of the South. In so doing they knew that they were courting certain political ostracism and defeat, subjecting themselves to danger and perhaps to death, and to what was equally terrible to men of their pride and character—the changing of the love and confidence of their neighbors and friends, and even their kindred, into bitter hatred; and yet these men through all those dreary, doubtful years of war, some at their homes, some in the mountains, some in exile, some in prison and others on the battle-field beneath the stars and stripes, never wavered or lost hope in the success of the one cause for which they had sacrificed and dared so much—the success of the Union arms.

Their voices were never heard among the croakers; when they could not approve the policy of the government, they fought on in silence; when colored troops were enlisted, they faltered not; when the Emancipation Proclamation swept away their fortunes, they did not complain. The success of one political party or the other was no victory to them, except as it indicated the determination of the people to preserve the government by suppressing the rebellion. They did not regard the war, as many writers do, as a "war between the North and South," or a "war between the States," but a war between those everywhere who loved their government and those who wished to see it die; and if their hearts were not too full of sadness to harbor bitter feelings, those feelings went out toward the Northern "Copper-head" rather than toward their misguided or even their vicious neighbors. They did not consider it a rebellion of State, but a rebellion of rebels. They knew that they were sustained in their own section by thousands of Southerners as courageous and patriotic as themselves, and by hundreds of thousands who, though unable to give them active support, were praying for success.

Next to their devotion to the Union their desire for peace, good government in the South through a liberal policy by the victorious party was the aim and hope of these men. Then came reconstruction and the reorganization of political parties in the South. It must be written that the National Republican party, controlled by Northern politicians, in the exercise of its powerful political influence and the bestowal of its great patronage, in every Southern State and in almost every instance rejected the counsel of these brave and experienced men, and sought tc build upon three elements only—the negro, the carpetbagger, and a few new converts from the Confederate element. This is the only blur upon the otherwise magnificent record of that party.

ENEMIES AND PHILOSOPHY.

In the summer of 1900 my brother, General Mills, and a sister paid Mrs. Mills and myself a visit at the United States Consulate at Chihuahua. One evening he, being in a reflective mood, said, "Will, you and I have had many difficulties, and quarrels and fights with our personal enemies, and it is very gratifying to know, as I am growing old, that these are all over with me. My enemies are all reconciled to me, and I wish you could say as much."

I replied: "I do not know that my enemies are all reconciled to me, but they are all *dead*, and that is better, or at least *safer*." And it is the literal truth. All my bitterest foes have been taken hence, most of them by violence, and I neither rejoice at nor regret their taking off. I do not claim that I was always right and they always wrong, for I tried to return blow for blow, but it is certain that they often resorted to means which I would, under no circumstances, employ. Alas, most of my friends are gone also. Why I have been spared through it all is a mystery which I do not attempt to explain.

A'DOIS.